Handbook of Textile Manufacturing

Handbook of Textile Manufacturing

– Author –
Aishwarya Basu
J.C. Bose

Wordpen Academics
Publishing Science That Matter

ISBN: 978-81-96302-53-5 (Hardback)

Published by : **WORDPEN ACADEMICS**
4736/23, Ansari Road, Darya Ganj,
New Delhi – 110 002
Phone: +91-011-35004336
E-mail: info@wordpenacademics.com

Printed at **:** **Replika Press Pvt. Ltd.**

Exclusive Distributor: ***Bio-Green Books, New Delhi***

Preface

Textile products play a vital role in meeting mans basic needs. We often only consider textiles to be the clothes we wear. Obviously, the clothing industry is where the majority of textiles are produced and used. However, textiles are also important in all aspects of our lives from death. The use of textiles has been traced back over 8500 years. The technological advances of textiles in various industries do not always get recognized as they do in the clothing industry. The following paragraphs describe some important roles that textiles play in other industries. Farmers wear protective clothing to spray their crops with pesticides. Textiles are used to cover plants and wrap trees for protection from weather and insects. Coffee filters and tea bags are made of a non-woven textile. The annual production of tea bag string would stretch around the equator 67 times. Textiles are used in our homes to insulate them from heat and cold. The furniture, on which we sit and sleep, is composed of various types of textile products. .

Textiles are used in roofing materials, wire coverings, wall coverings, blinds, air ducts and window screens. The transportation industry relies on textiles to line the beds of the roads before they are paved. A tire gets seventy five percent of its strength from textiles. Kevlar aramid is often used to strengthen radial tires because it is lightweight and five times stronger than steel. The interiors of all types of transportation vehicles are covered with textiles. Textiles are also used in the brake linings, gaskets, seals, seat belts, airbags and filters of vehicles. The Lear Fan Jet airplane body is composed of 100percent carbon fiber composite material. This carbon material is half the weight of aluminum and as strong as steel. The heat shields on spacecraft are composed of a fiber that will withstand 20,000 degrees Fahrenheit. Textiles are used as life saving devices in the healthcare industry. The artificial kidney used in dialysis is made of 7,000 hollow fibers and is only two inches in diameter. The Jarvik-7 artificial heart is composed of over fifty percent textiles and has Velcro fittings. Over 150,000 people in the United States have artificial arteries made of knitted polyester, which aids in preventing clotting and rejection. The invention of disposable clothing helps prevent the spread of bacteria. Sutures for wounds are now made of a dissolvable textile fiber. Casts for broken bones, surgical masks, bandages and gloves are other examples of textiles used in the healthcare industry.

The book provides an overview of various textile manufacturing processes. It covers the fundamental concepts and principles involved in the production of textiles, including fiber selection, spinning, weaving, knitting, dyeing, printing, and finishing. It serves as a foundation for understanding the subsequent chapters on garment manufacturing. It focuses on the seam performance of garments, which plays a crucial role in determining their durability and quality. It explores different types of seams used in garment construction, their characteristics, and factors affecting their strength and performance and discusses seam testing methods and standards to ensure the integrity of garment seams. Intimate apparel, such as lingerie and underwear, demands high levels of comfort for the wearer. It also delves into the innovations and advancements in materials, design, and construction techniques that enhance the comfort of intimate apparel. It covers topics like moisture management, breathability, flexibility, and ergonomic design principles specific to intimate garments. Textiles play a vital role in applications requiring specialized functionalities, such as protective clothing and equipment. This chapter specifically examines the design and development of stab-resistant body armor using the fused deposition modeling (FDM) process. It discusses the materials, structural features, and manufacturing considerations necessary to achieve effective stab resistance. The chapter also includes analysis techniques to evaluate the performance and effectiveness of such protective garments. The "Handbook of Textile Manufacturing" covers a wide range of topics related to garment manufacturing, yarn manufacturing, and technical textiles design and development. It provides valuable insights into the various processes, technologies, and innovations shaping the textile industry. With its comprehensive and in-depth approach, this handbook serves as a valuable resource for professionals, researchers, and students involved in textile manufacturing and related fields.

We are grateful to all those persons as well as various books, manuals, periodicals, magazines, journals etc. that helped in the preparation of this book. In spite of the best efforts, it is possible that some errors may have occurred into the compilation and editing of the book. Further queries, constructive suggestions and criticisms for the improvement of the book are always welcome and shall be thankfully acknowledged.

Aishwarya Basu
J.C. Bose

Contents

Section 1

Garment Manufacturing

Chapter 1

Introductory Chapter: Textile Manufacturing Processes

1. Introduction

Textile fibers provided an integral component in modern society and physical structure known for human comfort and sustainability. Man is a friend of fashion in nature. The desire for better garment and apparel resulted in the development of textile fiber production and textile manufacturing process.

Primarily the natural textile fibers meet the requirements for human consumption in terms of the comfort and aesthetic trends. Cotton, wool, and silk were the important natural fibers for human clothing articles, where cotton for its outstanding properties and versatile utilization was known as the King Cotton.

Cotton is an important natural fiber produced in Asian and American continent since the last around 5000 years in the countries including the USA, India, China, Turkey, Pakistan, Brazil, etc. [1]. The advancement of fiber manufacturing introduced several man-made fibers for conventional textile products; however, cotton is to date a leading textile fiber in home textiles and clothing articles. The chemistry of cotton fiber is the principal source of interesting and useful properties required in finished textile products [2]. Strength, softness, absorbency, dyeing and printing properties, comfort, air permeability, etc. are the important properties of cotton to remain an important textile fiber in the market. By 2018 cotton fiber was significant with a market share of 39.47% as raw material in textile products.

Cotton fiber grown with increased environment-friendly properties is called organic cotton. It is grown without using any synthetic chemicals or pesticides, fertilizers, etc. Organic cotton is produced through crop with the processing stages in an ecological environment. Turkey, the USA, and India are the main countries producing organic cotton.

The other important natural fibers used in conventional textile products are wool and silk. Wool fiber is known for its warmer properties and used mainly in winter wear mainly. Wool-based textile items are projected to witness a CAGR of 3.7%, in terms of volume, from 2019 to 2025. Importantly, wool fiber is renewable and recyclable, which supports its demand in this industry [3].

Silk fiber is known for its unmatchable softness and low linear density. Relative to cotton and wool, natural silk is not produced in significant quantity. It is indicated to have the highest revenue growth rate of 4.67% from 2019 to 2025.

A recent study of textile fiber market share by the IHS Markit has shown the synthetic fibers consumed highest (mainly represented by polyester and nylon fibers) followed by cotton, cellulosics, and wool fibers (**Figure 1**) [4]. China is the major manufacturer of synthetic fibers. Excluding polyolefin fibers, China produces around 66% of synthetic fibers in 2015.

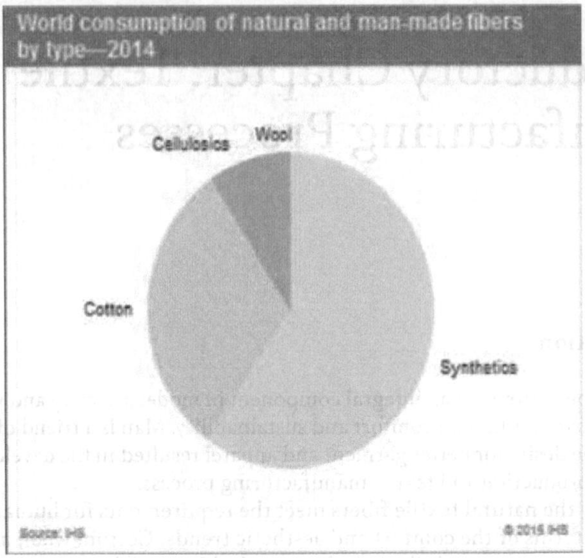

Figure 1.
Natural and man-made fibers consumed in the global textile market (IHS Markit [4]).

The textile manufacturing processes are largely required by the fashion segment in the global textile market. The large amount of textile products, demanded by fashion, accounted for more than 65% of textile product market. Fashion market is followed by technical textiles and household products. Grand View Research indicated fashion, technical textiles, and household as the top three sectors by application for the global textile market (**Figure 2**) [3].

Compound annual growth rate of 4.25% is expected over the years 2018–2025 in the global textile market. This market was estimated at USD 925.3 billion in 2018. The growth is significantly expected in the apparel sector. China and India will remain the leading countries to experience this growth. Increasing urban population with rising disposable income is the main source of higher growth in apparel consumption.

The textile manufacturing processes in the global textile industry are producing the textile yarn, fiber, fabric, and finished products including apparels. The global textile industry associated with the apparel and non-apparel products is expected

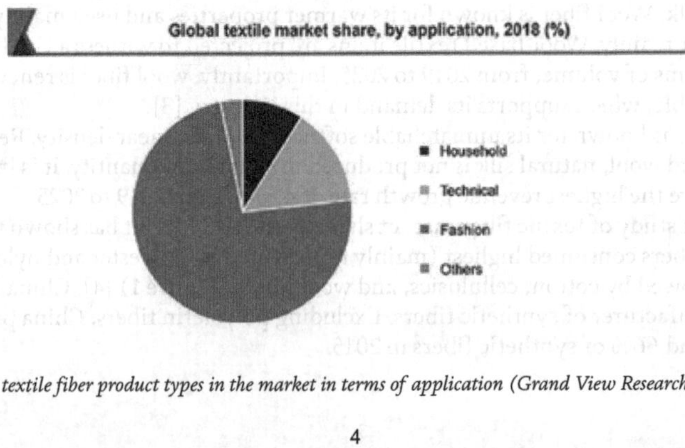

Figure 2.
Important textile fiber product types in the market in terms of application (Grand View Research) [3].

to exceed USD 1000 billion in the next couple of years [5]. The textile industry market is mainly represented by countries China, the USA, India, and the European Union. China is indicated as the country with leading textile manufacturing facility representing around one-fourth of the global textile industry.

An important aspect that has received increasing concern in textiles is the release of environmental hazard from fiber and fabric process industries. Most of the processes performed in textile manufacturing release significant toxic and hazard waste to river water, soil and air. Particularly fiber and yarn manufacturing, chemical finishing, pre-treatment processes, dyeing, printing, coating, and drying operations are releasing toxic gases, carcinogenic materials, harmful vapor and lint, and effluent discharge. Consequently, standards and regulations are evolved to limit or eliminate the environmental depreciation.

2. Textile manufacturing process

Today the textile industry encompasses a significant number and variety of processes that are adding value in fiber. These processes may range over the yarn making through the garment stitching, fabric embossing, and composite production. However, considering the textile fiber as the basic building unit of any textile product, the textile manufacturing may clearly be identified as the conventional and technical textiles.

The conventional textile manufacturing process has a long history of converting the natural fiber into useful products including fabric, home textiles, and apparel and more recently into a technical textile through the utilization of special finishing effects (**Figure 3**).

The synthetic and semisynthetic fiber manufacturing is diversified with the utilization of monomer, chemical agent, precursor, catalyst, and a variety of auxiliary chemicals resulting in the formation of fiber or yarn. However, such man-made

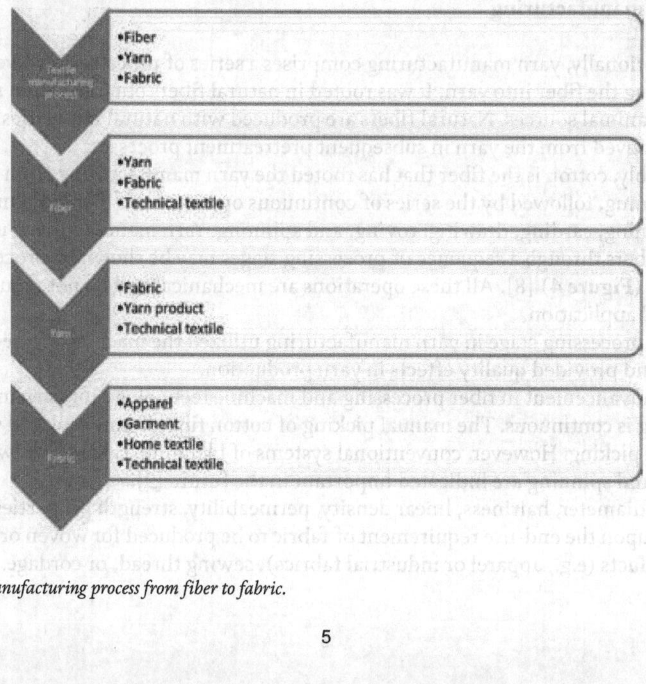

Figure 3.
Textile manufacturing process from fiber to fabric.

fibers are perceived as a separate specialized subject and beyond the scope of this book. Therefore, the man-made fiber manufacturing is not discussed.

The innovation in textile manufacturing introduced variety in raw materials and manufacturing processes. Therefore, process control to ensure product quality is desired. Monitoring and controlling of process parameters may introduce reduction in waste, costs, and environmental impact [6].

All the processing stages in textile manufacturing from fiber production to finished fabric are experiencing enhancement in process control and evaluation. It includes textile fiber production and processing through blow room, carding, drawing, and combing; and fabric production including knitted, woven, nonwoven, and subsequent coloration and finishing and apparel manufacturing.

The global textile industry, in yarn and fabric production, has strong presence and experiencing growth. In 2016, the yarn and fabric market was valued at USD 748.1 billion, where the fabric product was more in consumption and contributed 83.7% and the yarn product was at 16.3%. The market consumption is forecasted for growth at CAGR of 5.1% between 2016 and 2021, reaching to a market value of USD 961.0 billion in 2021 [7].

Apparel production is another important area in textile manufacturing around the textile industry chain. Probably the apparel is what an individual wear for the purpose of body coverage, beautification, or comfort. Apparel and garment terms are used interchangeably. However, the two terms may be differentiated as apparel is an outerwear clothing and garment is any piece of clothing.

The study of apparel manufacturing market includes all the clothing articles except leather, footwear, knitted product, and technical, household, and made-up items. The worldwide apparel manufacturing market was valued at USD 785.0 billion in 2016 and estimated to reach the level of USD 992 billion in 2021. The market enhancement is forecasted to move from 2016 to 2021 at CAGR of 4.8%.

3. Types of textile manufacturing process

3.1 Yarn manufacturing

Traditionally, yarn manufacturing comprises a series of processes involved in converting the fiber into yarn. It was rooted in natural fibers obtained from natural plant or animal sources. Natural fibers are produced with natural impurities that were removed from the yarn in subsequent pretreatment processes.

Possibly, cotton is the fiber that has rooted the yarn manufacturing from fiber bale opening, followed by the series of continuous operations of blending, mixing, cleaning, carding, drawing, roving, and spinning. Yarn manufacturing using cotton fibers through a sequence of processing stages may be shown by process flow diagram (**Figure 4**) [8]. All these operations are mechanical and do not require chemical application.

Each processing stage in yarn manufacturing utilized the machine of specialized nature and provided quality effects in yarn production.

The advancement in fiber processing and machine technology for yarn manufacturing is continuous. The manual picking of cotton fiber is now replaced with machine picking. However, conventional systems of blending, carding, drawing, roving, and spinning are indicated important in the future [9].

Yarn diameter, hairiness, linear density, permeability, strength properties, etc. depend upon the end-use requirement of fabric to be produced for woven or knitted end products (e.g., apparel or industrial fabrics), sewing thread, or cordage.

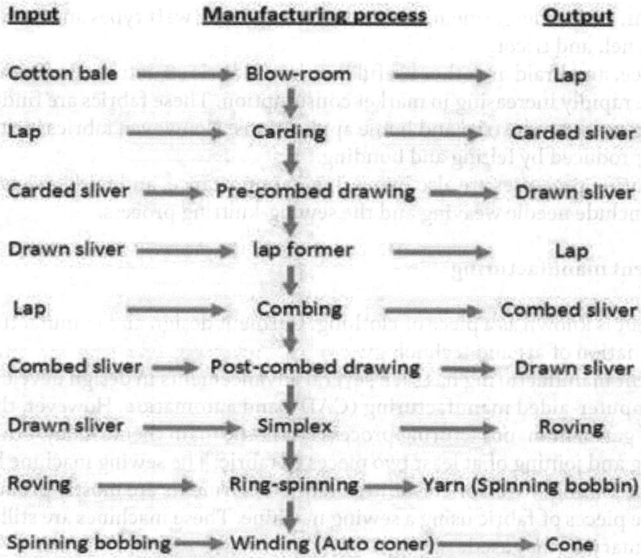

Figure 4.
Processing stages in cotton yarn manufacturing [8].

Several interesting works on the production of yarn are available that provide details of the material processing and technological control. Introductory spinning technology is described by Lawrence [10]. It covers the rudiments of staple-yarn technology, the manufacturing process, the raw materials, and the production processes for short-staple, worsted, semi-worsted, woolen spinning, doubling, and specialty yarn. Some of the useful advanced topics discussed are staple-yarn technology, including new development in fiber preparation technology, carding technology, roller drafting, ring spinning, open-end rotor spinning, and air-jet spinning.

Peter described the yarn production technology in combination with the economics [11]. The study is useful for yarn manufacturing and its development in the textile industry. Important topics covered include review of yarn production, filament yarn production, carding and prior processes for short-staple fibers, sliver preparation, short-staple spinning, long-staple spinning, post-spinning processes, quality control, and economics of staple-yarn production.

3.2 Fabric manufacturing

Textile fabric is at least a two-dimensional structure produced by fiber/yarn interlacing. The interlaced fibrous structure mainly used is woven, nonwoven, and knitted. Traditionally, the weaving technology was the principal source for fabric production.

The important types of woven fabric produced are the basic weaves, such as plain or tabby, twill, and satin, and the fancy weaves, including pile, jacquard, dobby, and gauze.

Knitted fabric is the second major type of fabric used following the woven. It has a characteristic of accommodating the body contour and provided the ease of movement. It is particularly a comfortable form of fabric structure for sports, casual wear, and undergarment. Knitted fabrics include weft types and the warp types, raschel, and tricot.

Net, lace, and braid are other useful interlaced fabric structures. Nonwoven fabrics are rapidly increasing in market consumption. These fabrics are finding interesting uses in industrial and home applications. Nonwoven fabrics include materials produced by felting and bonding.

Laminating processes are also increasing in importance, and fairly recent developments include needle weaving and the sewing-knitting process.

3.3 Garment manufacturing

Garment is known as a piece of clothing. Garment design and manufacturing is the combination of art and technology.

Garment manufacturing has seen several advancements in design development, computer-aided manufacturing (CAD), and automation. However, the older version of garment manufacturing process is still the main theme today—that is, the cutting and joining of at least two pieces of fabric. The sewing machine has the function of joining woven or cut-knitted fabrics. Garments are mostly produced by sewing the pieces of fabric using a sewing machine. These machines are still based on the primary format used.

Today the important topics in the current garment manufacturing industry range over product development, production planning, and material selection. The selection of garment design, including computer-aided design, spreading, cutting, and sewing; joining techniques; and seamless garment construction are beneficial in meeting the consumer needs. The development in finishing, quality control, and care-labeling of garment are meeting the point-of-sale requirements.

3.4 Technical textile

Technical textile is an established domain of interdisciplinary application of textile products. Most of the major industrial sectors are benefiting the function of fiber material.

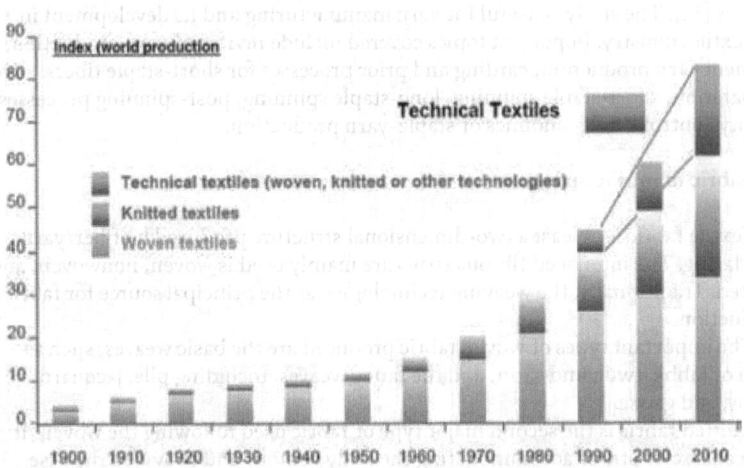

Figure 5.
Emergence of technical textile products from 1990 and its growth with knitted and woven textiles [12].

Any technical textile is a fibrous structure or a textile product that is produced for technical performance rather than fashion or aesthetic requirements.

Currently, technical textiles occupy strong market consumption. It is significantly an important sector for industrial development in industrialized and developing countries.

There are 12 types of technical textile with example product application which may be outlined as under:

- Meditech—sanitary diapers, bandages, sutures, mosquito nets, heart valves, ligaments, etc.
- AgroTech—crop protection net, bird protection, water tank, etc.
- BuildTech—ropes, tarpaulin, concrete reinforcement, window blind, wall covering, etc.
- MobileTech—car airbags, aircraft seats, boat, seat belt, etc.
- ProTech—protective gloves, knife and bulletproof vest, flame-retardant and chemical-resistant clothing, etc.
- InduTech—conveyor belts, cordage, filtration media, etc.
- HomeTech—sofa and furniture fabric, floor covering, mattresses, pillow, etc.
- ClothTech—sun shade, parachute fabric, sewing threads, interlinings, etc.
- SportTech—sports shoe, swimsuit, sports nets, sleeping bags, sail cloths, etc.
- PackTech—tea bags, wrapping fabrics, jute sacks, etc.
- OekoTech or EcoTech (textiles in environment protection)—erosion protection, air cleaning, prevention of water pollution, waste treatment/recycling, etc.
- Geotech—nets for seashore and geo structures, mats, grids, composites, etc.

The emergence of technical textile products was realized in the 1990s, in addition to the conventional woven and knitted textile articles. However, since then technical textiles showed phenomenal growth (**Figure 5**) [12].

More recently, the global technical textile market has shown significant growth in consumption, and it is estimated to continue in the future. Technical textile market was estimated at USD 165.51 billion in 2017 and is projected to reach USD 203.7 billion by 2022. The CAGR of from 2917 to 2022 is indicated 5.89%.

4. Value addition in textile manufacturing

4.1 Pretreatment process

Any of fiber substrate including fiber/yarn, fabric, garment, technical textile, etc. may require a series of chemical processing to reduce the undesired content from the fiber. The selection of any pretreatment process, its composition, and methodology depends upon the end-use requirement of the textile product.

A pretreatment process is generally required to introduce two important value additions in textile substrate including:

I. Removing the undesired content from the fiber mass including dust, coloring matters, undesired oils, lint, trash, etc.

II. Imparting the required level of fiber property for subsequent processing of textile substrate. The required fiber property may include fabric whiteness, absorbency, softness, strength, weight, width, etc.

The pretreatment processes performed in conventional textile industry are sizing, desizing, scouring, bleaching, mercerization, washing, and heat setting. One or more of any of these processes are required for the textile substrate depending upon the end use of the textile.

Traditionally, the pretreatment process is performed on cotton, cellulose fibers, wool, and the blend of these fibers with synthetics and semisynthetics. Natural fibers including cotton and wool have natural impurities, and the purpose of pretreatment is primarily to remove undesired natural fiber content.

4.2 Coloration process

Dyeing, printing, and coating are the coloration processes to produce beautiful motif and color effect on textile. Printing and coating are limited to surface coloration and may be applied to most of the fiber types, natural fabrics, and synthetics. Approximately 10,000 different dyes and pigments are used industrially around the world [13].

Dyeing is the coloring effect throughout the cross section of fiber, and this effect can be produced on any form of textile substrate including fiber/yarn, fabric, garment, and clothing articles. However, any dyestuff is suitable for a particular type of fiber for dyeing.

Dyeing of textile substrate is performed using any of the dyestuff including reactive, direct, sulfur, vat, pigment, acid, and disperse, depending upon the dye-fiber system compatibility. The dyeing method used can be continuous, semicontinuous, and batching. Continuous dyeing technique is performed for large-scale production in the industry.

Fixation of dyestuff in fabric or garment should be significantly fast during the service life to provide resistance and durability against washing, heat, chemicals, soaping, rubbing, sunlight, etc.

Washing of the dyed fabric and the discharge of dye effluent may release 10–50% of dyestuff to the environment [13], and that is the environmental concern associated with the dyeing process. Globally, the inefficient dyeing and finishing process may result in the release of 200,000 tons of used dyestuff to the environment.

4.3 Special finishing process

Special finishing effects are required in textile fibers. The functional attributes of textile fibers are limited. Textile products are required to exhibit a variety of performance effects for end use. Crease recovery, flame retardant, water repellent, antibacteria, antistatic, moth proofing, softening, and hand-builder are the special finishing effects that can be produced in textile.

Conventionally, special finishing is performed following the coloration of textile; however, innovation has shown the possibility of performing special finishing

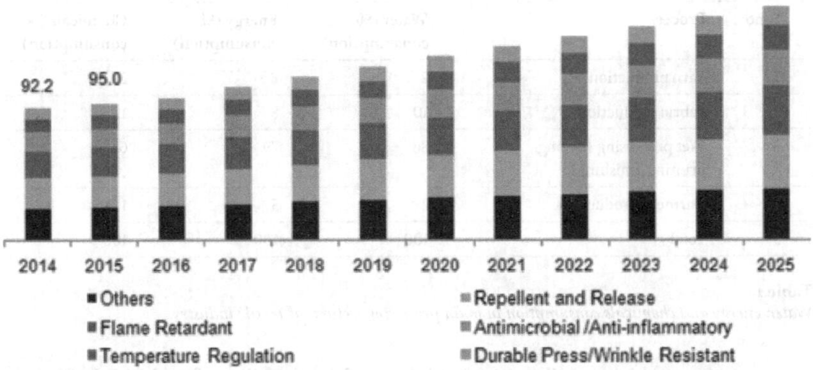

Figure 6.
Functional finish market growth (USD million) in the USA for 2014–2025 by product type (Grand View Research, USA [18]).

prior the coloration and special finishing in combination with the coloration process. The subject of investigating the alternating finishing and coloration processing sequences may offer the enhanced finish effects or coloration effects [14–17].

The global textile functional finishing is experiencing continuous growth, and the trend is forecasted to survive in the future. The market size was estimated at 114.2 million tons in 2015, and in terms of monetary value, it is expected to grow at a CAGR of 6.1% from 2016 to 2025 [18].

The USA is the major textile market for the consumption of special finishes. Grand View Research, USA, published future growth figures for special finishes that indicated almost all the important types of special finishes to rise in consumption till 2025 (**Figure 6**).

Over 50% supply of the special finishing agents is indicated to be through five major chemical companies including Dow Chemical Company; Bayer AG; BASF SE; Sumitomo Chemicals Co., Ltd.; and Huntsman International LLC. Asian countries including India, China, Bangladesh, and Vietnam are expected to see a flourishing market with the support of public policies.

Stronger environmental regulations, emission, and pollution control in the application, processing, and service life performance are the challenges in the use of special finishes [19].

5. Environment and textile manufacturing

All the environmental spheres, such as air, water and soil, are seriously affected by the textile manufacturing processes from fiber production to final fabric finishing. Consequently, a number of initiatives are introduced in textile industry by the public and private partnership to enhance the environment-friendly nature of textile processing.

Chemical used in fiber manufacturing and processing of textiles, effluent discharge from the textile dyeing, printing, and finishing, dust, short fibers, and lint released from the yarn manufacturing, volatiles and toxic gases released, etc., are the undesired effects to environment and human lives.

An estimation of the undesired effects to environment associated with the major processing units of textile industry can be presented based on the amount of consumption of chemicals, water and energy used. More the chemicals, water and

S. no	Process	Water (% consumption)	Energy (% consumption)	Chemicals (% consumption)
1	Yarn production	2	8	22
2	Fabric production	10	8	12
3	Wet processing (dyeing/ printing/finishing)	86	79	65
4	Garment production	2	5	1
5	Total	100	100	100

Table 1.
Water, energy and chemicals consumption in main processing sections of textile industry.

energy consumed in a textile process, higher is the possibility of undesired effects to our planet and living species breathing and breeding in the environment. **Table 1** shows an estimated percentage consumption of water, energy and chemicals in main textile processing sections.

Living species are directly or indirectly affected by the inhalation of toxic gases, consumption of contaminated water and food items, and the skin contact of toxic vapors and gases. The increasing realization of hazards associated with the textile manufacturing by the industrialized region in particular has resulted in the following important phenomena in textile sector:

1. conventional textile processing industries are clustered in developing countries;

2. technical textiles or textile processing with reduced environmental hazards grown in developed region; and

3. environmental standards, produced through the public and private participation, are increasing in practice in textile industries across the world to enhance the environment-friendly processes and products.

Water and chemicals are throughout the processing chain of textiles. Fiber manufacturing and processing, sizing, desizing, scouring, bleaching, mercerization, dyeing, printing, finishing etc., are known for water, chemical, and energy intensive nature. An increasing world population and the rising number of people to afford enhanced quantity of garments are elevating the production and processing of kilogram of fibers. Therefore, today, an individual is consuming more quantity of clothing, and there is an increasing population for higher consumption demand of clothing.

There may be than 1900 chemicals used in the production of clothing; where the European Union classified 165 the EU chemicals as hazardous to environment. An estimation made in 2015 for the assessment of environment hazard created by the global textile and clothing industry indicated the consumption of 79 billion of cubic meter of water. Large amount of this water is discharged into river and land without significant treatment in less developed countries. Toxic gaseous emission from textile processing is estimated to 1715 million tons of CO_2, and material waste is 92 million. If the processes continue in similar situation till 2030, the indicated water, gas and waste hazard will increase by at least 50% [20].

There are 107 eco-labels for textiles presently used [21]. In several developing countries, the textile processing industries are following the practice of ecolabels, and the voluntarily eco-standards to demonstrate the environment- friendly process and product. An important example is Oeko-Tex Series of Standards that may be briefly described as follows [22]:

I. STANDARD 100 by OEKO-TEX: It may be described as an independent testing and certification system for raw, semi-finished, and finished textile products through all the processing stages. This standard is particularly useful for legal regulations, for example on banned azo colorants, and harmful chemicals.

 OEKO-TEX 100 Standard helps the processor and producer of textile product to demonstrate the compliance for legal regulations including those limiting the banned azo colorants, formaldehyde, pentachlorophenol, cadmium, nickel, etc., and the voluntarily prevention of harmful chemicals that are not legally regulated.

II. SUSTAINABLE TEXTILE PRODUCTION (STeP) by OEKO-TEX® is a certification system for brands, retail companies and manufacturers in the textile chain to inform the public that they performed sustainable manufacturing processes. Therefore, STeP certification is applicable to all the sections of textile processing sector including fiber production, yarn manufacturing, fabric manufacturing, and garment production.

 Any processing unit certified with STeP Standard means it follows the environment- friendly processes, ensure health and safety practices, and implement socially sound working environment for all the staff and place.

III. ECO PASSPORT by OEKO-TEX® is another standard. It provided the testing and certification system for chemicals, colorants and auxiliaries used in the processing of textile fiber. A three-stage verification is exercised on chemicals applied in textile processing to demonstrate compliance to safety, sustainability and statutory regulation.

IV. DETOX TO ZERO by OEKO-TEX® is the standard to evaluate the chemical management system in the textile chain coupled with the waste water and sludge quality disposed to environment by a textile unit. This standard requires the verification through an independent source.

 Detox to Zero Status Report of a textile unit for chemical management and waste water and sludge control is based on providing the parameters including management system and organization structure, compliance to the legal requirements for storage and handling of chemicals, environmental protection, health and safety of employees, and production process.

6. Conclusion

Textile fibers provided an integral component in modern society and physical structure known for human comfort and sustainability. Man is an ancient friend of fashion. The quest for better garment and apparel led to the development of textile fiber production and textile manufacturing process.

A textile manufacturing process involves the production or conversion of textile fiber through a defined process in a product. The resultant textile product can be a finished product ready for consumer market, or it may be an intermediate product to be used as an input (raw material) substance to produce another textile product.

In general the conventional post-fiber formation processes may mainly be classified as physical and chemical textile manufacturing processes. A physical textile manufacturing process is required to convert the textile fiber into yarn; nonwoven, woven, knitted, technical textile; special finishing effects; etc. The chemical textile manufacturing processes include sizing, desizing, scouring, bleaching, mercerization, dyeing, printing, special chemical finishing, etc.

The chapters in this book are to share the development work in yarn manufacturing, fabric manufacturing, garment, and technical textiles. It is a collection of research and academic works in areas of textile manufacturing by the authors with expert background in the topic. The content may serve as a useful learning through the research work and the literature review as the subject tutorial.

References

[1] Uddin F. Cotton and textile vision. Pakistan Textile Journal. 2007;**56**(1):37-38

[2] Lewin M, editor. Cotton Fiber Chemistry and Technology. 1st ed. USA: CRC Press, Taylor & Francis Group, LLC; 2007. pp. 14-15. ISBN 10: 1-4200-4587-3

[3] Anon. Textile Market Size, Share & Trends Analysis Report By Raw Material (Wool, Chemical, Silk, Cotton), By Product (Natural Fibers, Polyester, Nylon), By Application (Technical, Fashion & Clothing, Household), and Segment Forecasts, 2019-2025. San Francisco, CA, United States: Grand View Research, Inc; 2019. p. 215. Available from: https://www.grandviewresearch.com/industry-analysis/textile-market [Accessed: June 6, 2019]

[4] Anon. Natural and Man-Made Fibers Overview. 2015. IHS Markit. Available from: https://ihsmarkit.com/products/fibers-chemical-economics-handbook.html [Accessed: June 7, 2019]

[5] Mohan J. Global Textile Industry: Recent Trends in the Market. 2019. Available from: https://medium.com/@jashimohan01/global-textile-industry-recent-trends-in-the-market-45d2d2b86392 [Accessed: June 1, 2019]

[6] Majumdar A, Das A, Alagirusamy R, Kothari VK, editors. Process Control in Textile Manufacturing. 1st ed. UK: Woodhead Publishing; 2012. p. 512. ISBN 9780857090270

[7] Lu S. Market Size of the Global Textile and Apparel Industry: 2016 to 2021/2022. 2019. Available from: https://shenglufashion.com/2018/12/18/market-size-of-the-global-textile-and-apparel-industry-2016-to-2021-2022/ [Accessed: June 1, 2019]

[8] Hossain I. Textileknowledge. Available from: https://textileknowledge.files.wordpress.com/2011/10/flow-chart-for-combed-yarn1.jpg [Accessed: June 8]

[9] Wakelyn JP. Cotton Yarn Manufacturing, Encyclopaedia of Occupational Health and Safety. 2011. Available from: http://iloencyclopaedia.org/component/k2/item/880-cotton-yarn-manufacturing [Accessed: June 8, 2019]

[10] Lawrence CA. Fundamentals of Spun Yarn Technology. 1st ed. UK: CRC Press; 2003. p. 552. ISBN 9781566768214

[11] Lord PR, editor. Handbook of Yarn Production. 1st ed. UK: Woodhead Publishing; 2003. p. 504. ISBN 9781855736962

[12] Anon. Technical Textile Market Overview by Global and Indian Perspective. 2018. Available from: https://www.textilemates.com/technical-textile-market-global-indian/ [Accessed: June 9, 2019]

[13] Chequer FMD, de Oliveira GAR, Ferraz ERA, Cardoso JC, Zanoni MVB, de Oliveira DP. Chapter 6: Textile dyes: Dyeing process and environmental impact. In: Eco-Friendly Textile Dyeing and Finishing. Rijeka, Croatia: IntechOpen; 2013. pp. 151-153

[14] Uddin F. Cationisation of cotton prior to the coloration process. International Dyer. 2003;**9**:28-30

[15] Uddin F, Lomas M. Catalyst systems for crease recovery finishing prior to pigment printing. Coloration Technology. 2004;**120**(3):254-259

[16] Uddin F, Lomas M. Combined crease recovery finishing and pigment printing. Coloration Technology. 2005, 2005;**121**:158-163

[17] Faheem Uddin, Mike Lomas, book: Novel Processing in Special Finishing and Printing of Textiles, 1st Edition 2010, Pub. VDM Verlag Dr. Muller Aktiengesellschaft & Co. KG (Germany).

[18] Anon. Functional Textile Finishing Agents Market by Product (Antimicrobial, Flame Retardant, Repellent and Release, Temperature Regulation, Durable Press/Wrinkle Resistant), By Region, Competitive Strategies, And Segment Forecasts, 2018-2025. Report ID: GVR-1-68038-432-1; Grand View Research; 2017. p. 135. Available from: https://www.grandviewresearch.com/industry-analysis/functional-textile-finishing-agents-market [Accessed: June 10, 2017]

[19] Uddin F. Environmental concerns in antimicrobial finishing of textiles. International Journal of Textile Science. 2014;3(1A):15-20

[20] Sajn N. Environmental Impact of Textile and Clothing Industry, European Parliamentary Research Service, Members' Research Service. PE 633.143. 2019. pp. 1-10

[21] Anon. Ecolabel Index; Vancouver, BC, Canada. 2019. Available from: http://www.ecolabelindex.com/ecolabels/?st=category,textiles [Accessed: June 14, 2019]

[22] Anon. OEKO-TEXR Inspiring Confidence. 2019. Available from: https://www.oeko-tex.com/en/business/certifications_and_services/ots_100/ots_100_start.xhtml [Accessed: June 5, 2019]

Chapter 2

Seam Performance of Garments

Abstract

Seams are basic requirements in the manufacturing of garments. In general, seam performance has a great influence on the garment quality. Seam and stitch types affect the quality and appearance of garments. Seams of the garment must be durable and smooth. Stitch and seam types and stitch and seam parameters should be selected according to the garment and fabric type. Appearance and performance of the seams are dependent upon the stitch and seam types, stitch and seam parameters, seam defects and damages. Seam performance of a garment also depends on structural and mechanical properties of the fabric and strength, extensibility, security, durability, appearance and efficiency of the seams. In this study, the importance of the seam performance of garments is investigated. In this context, stitch and seam types used in garments are explained. However, the stitch and seam parameters, sewing needle penetration force, needle damage index, seam defects and damages that are effective at seam performance have been explained and their relations with each other are compared.

Keywords: garment, quality, seam, stitch, performance

1. Introduction

In recent years, more importance is given to quality, comfort and fit of the garment in the clothing industry. The most important features expected from a garment are its performance, durability, serviceability, aesthetic and conformance. Design and aesthetic appearance is very important for customers. Pattern, colour and fabric structure affect the design and aesthetic appearance of a garment.

Comfort is one of the most important parameters of clothing. Thermophysiological aspects, sensorial or tactile aspect, physiological aspect and fitting comfort are four basic elements for clothing comfort [1]. Fitting is a crucial factor of wearing comfort [2, 3]. The fitting comfort of the garment in use mainly depends on the elasticity of the seam. Stitch type, seam type, sewing thread type and stitch density affect the fitting comfort of the garment. Some of the manufacturers select stitch classes, stitch densities and sewing threads without consideration to their influence on the fitting comfort of the garment. It is therefore very important to select appropriate seam and stitch types in terms of fitting comfort [4].

Consumers want that the apparel must be fit to their bodies. Size of the garment does not be large or small to their bodies. Fitness is directly related to the pattern design, sizing, fabric structure and seams used to contour curves of the body. There are different fit-types for garment items that range from the slim and form-fitting to oversized [5].

Seam and stitch types are one of the most important elements in joining the patterns and giving a form to the garment. Seam and stitch types directly affect the quality, comfort and fitness of the garment. Choosing a stitch or seam type that is not suitable for garment reduces the quality, comfort and fitness of the garment. Appearance and performance of the seams are dependent upon the stitch and seam types, stitch densities, sewing machine settings and quality of sewing threads. Seam performance of a garment depends on fabric structural and mechanical properties and strength, extensibility, security, durability, appearance and efficiency of the seams.

In this study, it is planned to explain the importance of the seam performance of garments. In this context, stitch and seam types used in garments are explained. However, the parameters like seam strength, extensibility, seam slippage, sewing needle penetration force, seam appearance and seam efficiency that are effective at seam performance are examined.

2. Stitch and seam types

Suitable stitch and seam types should be selected when sewing a garment. Stitch and seam types which are not selected properly affect the sewing performance negatively.

The tensile characteristics of seamed fabric changes with the change of fabric bias angle of stitching and stitch densities. Some of the seams on a garment are not subjected to high levels of stress or extension in use, like the shoulder seams on a jacket. In contrast, some seams, such as arm joint seams and seams at the crotch area of the trousers are subjected to high levels of stretching in wear [6]. Therefore, high strength seams are preferred in these areas.

2.1 Stitch types

Stitch is defined as a loop of thread or yarn resulting from the single pass or movement of the needle in sewing. Stitch types are shown as a numerical designation relating to the essential characteristics of the interlacing of sewing thread in a stitch. Standards are very important in determining stitch types. Six stitch types are specified in the ASTM D 6193-16 'Standard Practices for Stitches and Seams' standard [7]. Stitch types are shown in **Table 1**.

Figures of six stitch types are shown in **Figure 1**. Stitch type 101 is formed with one needle thread which passes through the material and interlooped with itself on the undersurface of the material. Stitch type 100 has five different subgroups.

Stitch type 201 is formed with two needle threads which passed through the material in the same perforations from opposite directions without interlacing or interlooping. Stitch type 200 has five different subgroups.

Stitch class	Stitch type	Subgroup numbers of seam types	Subgroups of stitch types
100	Chain stitch with one needle thread	5	101–105
200	Hand stitch	5	201–205
300	Lockstitch	16	301–316
400	Multi Thread chain stitch	11	401–411
500	Overlock stitch	22	501–522
600	Covering chain stitch	10	601–610

Table 1.
Stitch types [7].

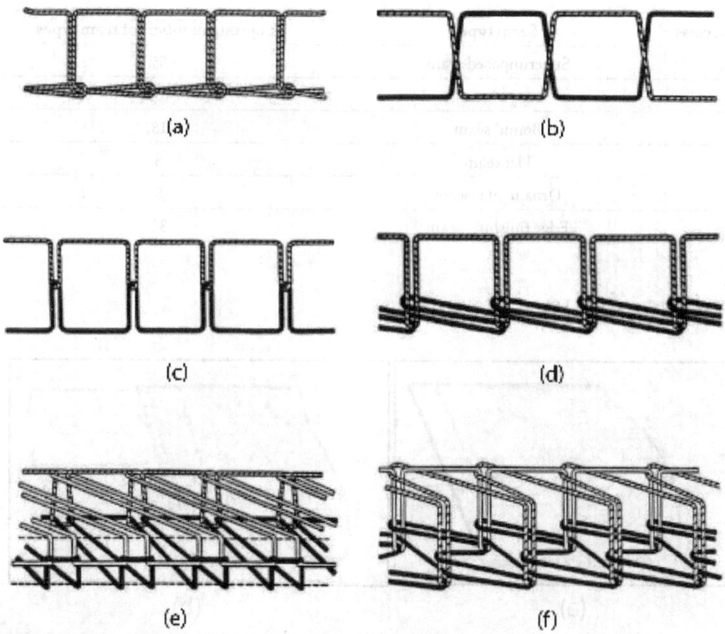

Figure 1.
Stitch types [7]: (a) stitch type 101; (b) stitch type 201; (c) stitch type 301; (d) stitch type 401; (e) stitch type 504; and (f) stitch type 601.

Stitch type 301 is formed with two threads, one needle thread and one bobbin thread. Loops of needle thread are passed through the material and interlaced with the bobbin thread. Needle thread is pulled back so that the interlacing was midway between surfaces of the materials being sewn. Stitch type 300 has 16 different subgroups.

Stitch type 401 is formed with two threads; one needle thread and one looper thread. Loops of needle thread are passed through the material and interlaced and interlooped with loops of bobbin thread. Interlooping was drawn against the underside of the bottom ply of the material. Stitch type 400 has 11 different subgroups.

Stitch type 504 is formed with three threads; one needle thread, one looper thread and one cover thread. Stitch type 500 has 22 different subgroups.

Stitch type 601 is formed three threads; two needle threads and one looper thread. Loops of the needle threads are passed through the material where they are looped with looper thread on the underside. Stitch type 600 has 10 different subgroups [7].

2.2 Seam types

The seam is defined as a juncture at which two or more planar structures, such as textile fabrics, are joined by sewing, usually near the edge. Seam types are shown as an alphanumeric designation relating to the essential characteristics of fabric positioning and rows of stitching in a seam. Standards are very important in determining seam types. Six seam types are specified in the ASTM D 6193-16 'Standard Practices for Stitches and Seams' standard [7]. Seam types are shown in **Table 2**.

Figures of six seam types are shown in **Figure 2**. Seam type SSa-2 is formed by superimposing two or more plies of material and seaming them with one or more

Seam class	Seam type	Subgroup numbers of seam types
SS	Superimposed seam	55
LS	Lapped seam	101
BS	Bound seam	18
FS	Flat seam	6
OS	Ornamental seam	8
EF	Edge finishing seam	32

Table 2.
Seam types [7].

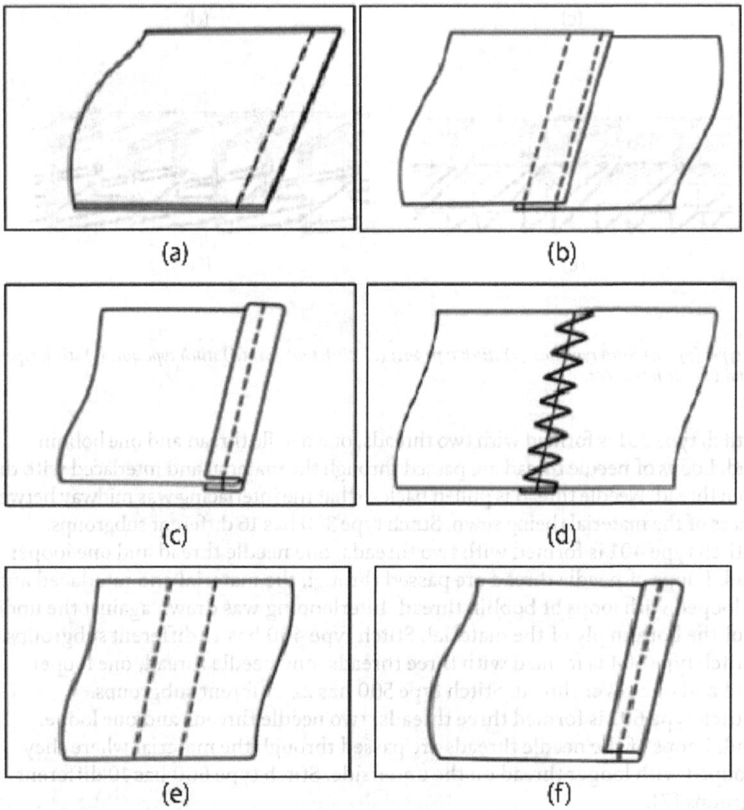

Figure 2.
Seam types [7]: (a) SSa-1; (b) LSa-1; (c) BSa-1; (d) FSc-1; (e) OSa-2; and (f)-EFa-1.

rows of 301 or 401 stitches a specified distance from their edges. Seam type SS (superimposed seam) has 55 different subgroups.

Seam type LSa-1 is formed by overlapping two or more plies of material a specified distance and seaming with one or more rows of stitches. Seam type LS (lapped seam) has 101 different subgroups.

Seam type BSa-1 is formed by folding a binding strip over the edge of the ply or plies of body material and seaming the binding strip and body material with one or more rows of stitches. Seam type BS (bound seam) has 18 different subgroups.

Seam type FSc-1 is formed by turning and abutting the turned edges of two plies of material and seaming with a row of stitches extending across and covering the turned edges of the material. Seam type FS (flat seam) has six different subgroups.

Seam type OSa-2 is produced with one or more straight rows of stitches. Seam type OS (ornamental seam) has eight different subgroups.

Seam type EFa-1 is produced by turning the edge of the material and stitching the turned portion to the body of the material with one or more rows of stitches. EF (edge finishing seam) seam type has 32 different subgroups [7].

Eight seam types are specified in ISO 4916:1991 'Textiles-Seam Types-Classification and Terminology' standard, which are as follows: Class 1—Superimposed seam, Class 2—Lapped seam, Class 3—Bound seams, Class 4—Flat seams, Class 5—Decorative/Ornamental stitching, Class 6—Edge finishing/neatening, Class 7—Attaching of separate items, Class 8—Single ply construction, Class 7—Attaching of separate items and Class 8—Single ply construction [8].

3. Stitch and seam parameters

3.1 Stitch density (SPI)

Stitch density is the number of stitches per unit length (stitch per inch-SPI) in one row of stitching in the seam. A higher SPI indicates greater stitch density and often higher quality stitching. In general, the more thread consumed in a stitch, the stronger the seam.

Stitches in the 6–8 per inch range convey a more primitive quilting style, suitable for heavy thread or utility quilts. Stitch 10–12 per inch is considered normal for most quilting styles and yields the best stitch quality as well. Longer stitch lengths create needle flex and increase tension changes. The average stitch length is 2.5 mm. This is the typical setting on the sewing machines. The equivalent of 2.5 mm is about 10–12 stitches per inch.

3.2 Stitch width

Stitch width is the distance between the lines of the outer most parts of the stitches. The stitch width determines how far the stitch will go from side to side.

A straight stitch like lockstitch has length but not width. The standard range for a lockstitch is stitch length 2.5 mm and stitch width 0. A zig-zag stitch or overlock stitch has length and width. The middle range of the stitch length for a zig-zag stitch is 2.5 mm and stitch width is 3 or 4 mm. Decorative stitches also have both length and width.

3.3 Seam allowance

Seam allowance is the area between the edge and the stitching line on two or more pieces of material being stitched together. Seam allowances can range from 1/4 inch (6.4 mm) wide to as much as several inches.

Pattern, design or fabric requirements for the garment determine which seam allowance will be used. A 5/8 inch (1.5 cm) seam allowance is generally considered a standard. For curved areas, such as necklines or armholes, the seam allowance may be only ¼ inch. But in areas that need extra fabric for the final fitting for the wearer seam allowances can be 1 inch or more.

3.4 Stitch length

The range of the stitch length is between 0 and 5 mm on most sewing machines. The average stitch length is 2.5 mm. The equivalent of 2.5 mm is about 10–12 stitches per inch. When stitch length increased, stitch density decreased.

Sewing machines indicate stitch length in millimetres. 2.5 mm stitch length means each stitch will be 2.5 mm long.

The short stitch length will be packed into each inch of stitching, creating a tighter seam. The long stitch length, the fewer each inch, therefore the looser the seam.

Stitches with long stitch lengths are holding the fabric together with less tension. These stitches are also better on thicker fabrics or when sewing through multiple layers.

3.5 Seam thickness

Seam thickness is used as a measure of seam pucker [9]. Seam thickness decreased as thread tensions and linear stitch density increased.

Eq. (1) was used to calculate the seam thickness [9, 10].

$$\Sigma t = 100\ (ts–2tf)/2tf \qquad (1)$$

where ts is the seam thickness and 2tf is the fabric thickness.

3.6 Seam extensibility

In recent years, the elasticity of the seam has become more important with the use of stretched fabrics in the garment.

Extensibility of the seamed fabric was defined as the difference in stitch length between the original stitch length S and the extended stitch length S_{lim}.

Eq. (2) was used to calculate the seam extensibility [11].

$$\text{Seam extensibility} = (S_{lim}–S)/S \qquad (2)$$

where S is the original stitch length and S_{lim} is the extended stitch length.

The elasticity of a sewn seam should be slightly greater than that of the material which it joins. This will enable the material to support its share of the forces encountered for the intended end use of the sewn item. The elasticity of a sewn seam depends on fabric type and strength, stitch and seam type, stitch density (SPI) and sewing thread elasticity [7].

Increasing the stitch density helps to increase stitch extensibility. An improvement in the stretch performance of a seam can be achieved by a balanced stitch.

3.7 Seam strength

Different types of garments have different seam strength requirements. Many factors affect the level of seam strength. These are fabric structure and properties, stress location of a garment, sewing thread type and construction, sewing machine tension, sewing needle type, stitch and seam types and stitch density [12]. It was observed that in woven and knitted fabrics, the seam strength increased when the number of stitches/cm and sewing thread size increased [13].

Seam strength can be measured according to ASTM D 1683-81 'Standard Test Method for Failure in Sewn Seams of Woven Apparel Fabrics'. This test method measures the sewn seams strength in woven fabrics by applying a force perpendicular to the sewn seams [14].

Seam strength depends on the thread strength and stitch density. Seam performance of the garment depends on the fabric cover factor, fabric weight, thickness, tensile strength, fabric shrinkage along the fabric length and width, resiliency, bending rigidity, flexural rigidity and shear rigidity [15].

Seam strength affects the functional and aesthetic performance of a garment and is important to its durability. Different seam angles affect seam strength too.

3.8 Seam efficiency

Seam efficiency is defined as the capacity of the material itself to carry a seam.

Seam efficiency is the ratio of seam strength to fabric strength. Eq. (3) was used to calculate the seam efficiency [10, 16].

$$\text{Seam efficiency} = 100 \times (\text{Seamed fabric strength}/\text{Unseamed fabric strength}) \quad (3)$$

The durability of the seam can be measured in terms of seam efficiency. Stitch efficiency can be optimized through various factors, such as fabric structure, seam type, type and density of stitches and the selection of sewing threads and needles. Seam efficiencies of 60–80% are common but efficiencies between 80 and 90% are more difficult obtaining from garment seams. Low seam efficiency values indicate that the sewn fabric is damaged during sewing.

4. Factors affecting seam performance

Seams are basic requirements in the garments. The characteristics of a properly constructed seam are its strength, elasticity, durability, stability and appearance, which depend on the seam type, stitches per unit length, the thread tension and the seam efficiency of the fabric [17]. Experience has shown that if the seam efficiency ratio falls below 80%, the fabric has been excessively damaged by the sewing operation [18].

Needle penetration force is one of the most important factors affecting the seam performance of a sewn garment. Sewing needle-related damage due to sewing in fabrics is another important factor affecting seam performance.

4.1 Sewing needle penetration force

The quantitative value of the needle penetration force is important in the manner of determining sewing damages that can appear in the sewing process on the fabric and is an important influence on the quality of the garment [19]. A high sewing needle penetration force means that the fabric has a high resistance and so there is a high risk of damage. Sewing needle penetration force and fabric deformation during sewing are effective factors for seam performance.

L&M Sewability tester is used for measurement sewing needle penetration force. The L&M Sewability tester enabled consecutive readings of force for penetration of fabric by a selected needle without sewing thread at a rate of 100 rpm. The fabric specimens were 30–40 mm wide and 350 mm length and a minimum of 100 perforations must be carried out [17]. If the penetration force did not exceed set level 75 cN, then the sewability value was zero, and sewability was considered to be very good. When sewability values ranged between 0 and 10%, the fabric sewability was considered good; between 10 and 20%, even though no great difficulties arose during sewing, the sewability was considered fair [20].

Lots of studies were done about needle penetration force. A study observed that needle penetration force values in both the warp and weft direction of the plain woven fabrics were higher than twill woven fabrics because of the plain dense structure. Sewing needle penetration force was affected by the weave type, yarn type and fabric density. While the fabric density increased, the needle penetration forces increased [17].

4.2 Sewing needle-related damage due to sewing in fabric

The sewing machine needles caused damages when a sewn seam assembly is used for a woven fabric. Sewing needle-related damage affected the seam performance by decreasing the seam strength. Needle-related damage due to sewing in woven fabrics can be measured according to ASTM D 1908-89 'The Needle-Related Damage due to Sewing in Woven Fabric' standard. Eq. (4) was used to calculate the needle damage index [19].

$$ND\% = 100\ (Ny/Pn) \quad (4)$$

where ND is the needle damage index due to fusing, severance or deflection (%), Ny is the number of yarns damaged in the direction evaluated and Pn is the number of needle penetrations.

This test method provides for determining a ratio of either the damaged yarns to the total number of yarns present in a seam assembly or the damaged yarns to the total number of needle penetrations.

There are lots of parameters that have an influence on the needle-related damage due to sewing in a fabric. These are fabric construction (yarn construction, structure, tightness, etc.), chemical treatments of the fabric (softness, dyes, finishing, washing), sewing needle number, design and sewing machine settings [12].

4.3 Seam defects and damages

4.3.1 Seam defects

Seam defects affect seam performance. Broken, skipped or missing stitches and seam pucker occur during the sewing process. Seam slippage and seam grinning are the other defects that occur during wearing the clothes. These defects are usually attributed to either a fault with the sewing machine, improper material or a worker error.

4.3.1.1 Seam slippage

Seam slippage is defined as that which occurs when the yarns in the fabric pull out of the seam at the edge or, alternatively, where the threads of a fabric begin to pull away from the stitching in a seam [12].

Resistance to slippage of yarns in woven fabrics can be measured according to ASTM D 434-75 'Resistance to Slippage of Yarns in Woven Fabrics Using a Standard Seam' standard [6]. This method covers the determination of the resistance to slippage of weft yarns over warp yarns, or warp yarns over weft yarns, using a standard seam.

Fibre, yarn and fabric composition, structure and properties and their processing parameters, finishing, laundering and seam allowance are affected seam slippage. Seam slippage can also occur because of the stress location of a garment, thread type and properties, sewing needle, stitch type, stitch density, seam type and sewing machine condition. Flexibility of the fabric is affected seam slippage too [12, 21].

4.3.1.2 Seam grinning

The seam grinning is defined as that when two pieces of fabric are pulled at right angles to the seam, a gap is revealed between the two pieces of the fabric revealing the thread in the gap. When a seam is loaded perpendicular to the direction of stitch line it tends to grin.

It was observed that seam grinning on the sewn fabric increased with decreased stitch density and increased thread extensibility. The seam grinning also increased as the fabric becomes rigid against deformation [22].

4.3.1.3 Seam pucker

Seam pucker is a wrinkled appearance along the seam, which influences the appearance of the garment. Seam pucker is usually caused by improper selection of seam parameters and fabric properties in the garment production.

In subjective evaluation method, experts or experienced judges grade the fabric seam appearance according to certain standards. According to AATCC 88B 'Smoothness of Seams in Fabrics after Repeated Home Laundering' standard, seam appearance is classified into five grades: grade 1 refers to the worst fabric which is heavily puckered and grade 5 refers to smooth fabric with little pucker or no pucker at all. **Figure 3** illustrates the photographs of reference seam specimens from AATCC 88B [23].

The sample fabrics are sewn as per standard procedures, and the appearance of the seam is compared with standard reference specimens. The grade of fabric is the grade of the reference specimen which matches most nearly to sample fabric specimen [24].

Puckering is usually caused by one or more of the following conditions:

- yarn displacement (structural compression of fabric yarns),
- tension puckering (excessive sewing thread extension and recovery),

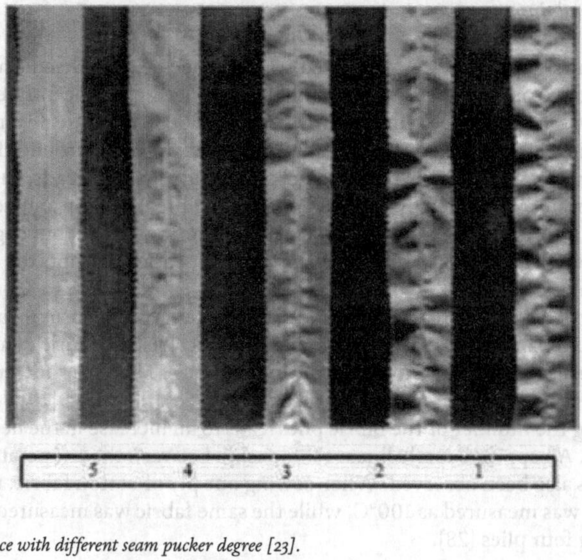

Figure 3.
Seam appearance with different seam pucker degree [23].

- feeding pucker (irregular feeding of fabric ply), and
- fabric and sewing thread shrinkage.

In recent years, many techniques have been developed by researchers to measure seam pucker. Subjective and objective techniques are the most common techniques to measure seam pucker. Eq. (5) was used to calculate the seam pucker percentage [24].

$$SP\% = (L_2 - L_1)/L_1 \times 100 \tag{5}$$

where SP% is the seam pucker percentage, L_1 is the length of sewn fabric and L_2 is the length of unravelled fabric.

According to Eq. (5), the difference between original length and puckered length gives a percentage for seam pucker.

Researchers used photometric instruments, computer vision, shadows by parallel light, laser triangulation, fractal geometry, artificial neural network and neurofuzzy logic methods to measure seam pucker [24].

4.3.2 Seam damages

Seam damages affect seam performance by reducing seam strength. The sewing damages can be occurred by high needle temperature, high pressure on pressure foot, unbalanced tension in sewing threads, irregular feeding system under the feed dog and sewing speed variation. Selection proper needle size and needle shape, thread lubrication ratio and sewing machine setting parameters can reduce seam damages during the process of sewing. Seam damages occur with thermal and mechanical damages. Seam damages are caused when fabric restricts the penetration of the sewing needle. This not only depends upon the spaces in the fabric, but also on needle profile, needle size, sewing machine setting and sewing thread [21, 25]. Fabric structure has an important effect on seam damages too [26].

4.3.2.1 Thermal damages

During the stitching, heat is dissipated from the needle. High needle heat causes thermal damages on the fabric. The heat held by the needle is concentrated in a small mass of metal, and the temperature can reach 300–350°C. Heat is transferred through the needle-bar to other sewing machine parts, to fabric around the needle, and to the sewing thread in the needle. Thermoplastic sewing threads, such as nylon and polyester, may be heated by the needle, melt and break. Nylon and polyester threads melt at 240–260°C. Cotton and silk are not thermoplastic, but degrade at around 400°C. Sewing thread breaks during sewing process disrupts the continuity of sewing process [27].

Sewing speed has the greatest influence on the needle temperature. Fabric-needle surface characteristics, fabric frictional characteristics, fabric density and thickness are also significant on the needle temperature. These parameters determine whether the needle temperature will be increased or lowered [10].

Increasing the number of the fabric plies leads to an increase in the needle temperature. An approximately linear relationship between the temperature and thickness has also been observed. When sewing one ply of cotton fabric, the needle temperature was measured as 100°C, while the same fabric was measured at 245°C when sewing four plies [28].

4.3.2.2 Mechanical damages

Mechanical damages affect the aesthetics and performance of the garment. During the stitching, fabric may be damaged by a sewing needle mechanically. In the case of mechanical damage, the yarns of the fabric are broken or fragmented. Such damages may be apparent immediately after stitching but frequently will not appear until after the product has been used, that is, when seams have been subjected to some form of tension, stress, strain, deformation or after successive cleaning.

Machine variables such as needle size, needle point design; material variables such as fabric structural properties, fabric finishing process causes mechanical damage [10].

It is critical to choose the correct sewing needle size for the correct sewing machine, sewing thread and fabric weight. Selection of correct sewing needle size is critical to the success of a quality sewn seam. The sewing thread selected for the garment should move freely through the eye of the selected sewing needle to ensure smooth passage during sewing.

Appropriate sewing needle size according to the sewing thread ticket number and fabric weight should be selected to prevent mechanical seam damages. Finer needle size, bulged-eye needles and lower sewing speed can reduce mechanical sewing damage [29, 30].

5. Conclusion

Seams are basic requirements in the manufacturing of garments. In general, seam performance has a great influence on garment products. Seam and stitch types affect the quality and appearance of garments.

Appearance and performance of the seams are dependent upon the stitch and seam types, stitch and seam parameters like stitch density, stitch width, seam allowance, stitch length, seam thickness, seam extensibility, seam strength, seam efficiency, sewing needle penetration force, sewing needle-related damage due to sewing and seam defects and damages.

Seam performance of a garment also depends on structural and mechanical properties of the fabric and strength, extensibility, security, durability, appearance and efficiency of the seams.

Seam strength and seam efficiency should be tested to determine the effect of sewing parameters on sewing performance. Seam defects and damages affect seam performance by making negative effects on sewing. Needle penetration force is one of the most important factors affecting the seam efficiency of a sewn garment. A high sewing needle penetration force means that the fabric has a high resistance and so there is a high risk of damage. Sewing needle-related damage due to sewing in fabrics is another important factor affecting seam efficiency.

Seams of the garment must be durable and smooth. Stitch and seam types and stitch and seam parameters should be selected according to the garment and fabric type. Stitches and seam types are very important for garment quality. Stitches are used to join the patterns of the garment, and seams give the shape and detail of the garment.

Standards are very important in determining stitch types. Six stitch types are specified in the ASTM D 6193-97 'Standard Practices for Stitches' standard. Six seam types are specified in the ASTM D 6193-97 'Standard Practices for Stitches' standard and eight seam types are specified in ISO 4916:1991 'Textiles-Seam Types-Classification and Terminology' standard.

Seam efficiency is defined as the capacity of the material itself to carry a seam.

Seam efficiencies of 60–80% are common, but efficiencies between 80 and 90% are more difficult obtaining from garment seams. Low seam efficiency values indicate that the sewn fabric is damaged during sewing.

Seam slippage, seam grinning and seam pucker is important seam defects, which influences the appearance of the garment. Seam defects are usually caused by improper selection of seam parameters and fabric properties in the garment production.

Seam damages affect seam performance by reducing seam strength. Thermal and mechanical damages affect the aesthetics and performance of the garment.

Appropriate sewing needle size according to the sewing thread ticket number and fabric weight should be selected to prevent mechanical seam damages.

Stitch and seam types and seam parameters must be selected correctly in order to obtain a quality seam.

References

[1] Das A, Alagirusamy R. Science in Clothing Comfort. India: Woodhead Publishing India PVT Ltd; 2010. 185p. ISBN: 788190800150

[2] Pechoux BL, Ghosh LD. Apparel Sizing and Fit. UK: The Textile Institute; 2002. p. 11

[3] Song G. Improving Comfort in Clothing. USA: Woodhead Publishing; 2011. 459p. ISBN: 978-1-84569-539-2

[4] Ukponmwan JO, Mukhopadhyay A, Chatterjee KN. Sewing threads. Textile Progress. 2000;**30**(3/4):91. DOI: 10.1080/00405160008688888

[5] Bubonia JE. Apparel Quality. USA: Fairchild Books; 2014. 232p. ISBN-13: 978-1628924572

[6] American Society for Testing and Materials - ASTM D 434-75. Resistance to slippage of yarns in woven fabrics using a standard seam. In: Annual Book of ASTM Standards. USA: Easton; 1975

[7] American Society for Testing and Materials - ASTM D 6193-16. Standard practices for stitches and seams. In: Annual Book of ASTM Standards. USA: Easton; 2016

[8] International Organization for Standardization - ISO 4916:1991. Textiles-Seam Types-Classification and Terminology. Switzerland; 1991

[9] Amirbayat J. Seams of different ply properties. Part I: Seam appearance. Journal of the Textile Institute. 1992;**83**:209-217. DOI: 10.1080/00405009208631191

[10] Laing RM, Webster J. Stitches and Seams. UK: The Textile Institute; 1998. 141p. ISBN: 1870812735

[11] O'Dwyer U, Munden DL. A study of the lockstitch seams, part I: A study of factors affecting the dimensions and thread consumption in lockstitch seams. Clothing Research Journal. 1975;**3**:33-40

[12] Fan J, Hunter L. Engineering Apparel Fabrics and Garments. UK: Woodhead Publishing; 2009. 416p. eBook ISBN: 9781845696443

[13] Amirbayat J. Seams of different ply properties part II: Seam strength. The Journal of the Textile Institute. 1994;**84**(1):31-38

[14] American Society for Testing and Materials - ASTM D 1683-81. Standard test method for failure in sewn seams of woven fabrics. In: Annual Book of ASTM Standards. USA: Easton; 1981

[15] Rajput B, Kakde M, Gulhane S, Mohite S, Raichurkar PP. Effect of sewing parameters on seam strength and seam efficiency. Trends in Textile Engineering and Fashion Technology. 2018;**4**(1):4-5. DOI: 10.31031/TTEFT.2018.04.000577

[16] Burtonwood B, Chamberlain NH. The Strength of Seams in Woven Fabrics: Part I. Clothing Institute Technology. Report No. 17; 1966

[17] Gurarda A, Meric B. Sewing needle penetration forces and elastane fiber damage during the sewing of cotton/elastane woven fabrics. Textile Research Journal. 2005;**75**(8):628-633. DOI: 10.1177/0040517505057640

[18] Mehta VH. An Introduction of Quality Control for the Apparel Industry. Milwaukee, Wisconsin, USA: ASQC; 1992. pp. 88-89

[19] American Society for Testing and Materials-ASTM D 1908-89. The needle-related damage due to sewing in woven fabric: In: Annual Book of ASTM Standards. USA: Easton; 1990

[20] Manich M, Domingues JP, Sauri RM, Barella A. Relationships between fabric sewability and structural, physical and fast properties of woven wool and wool-blended fabrics. Journal of the Textile Institute. 1998;**89**(3):579-589

[21] Choudhary AK, Sikka M, Bansal P. The study of sewing damages and defects in garment. Research Journal of Textile and Apparel. 2018;**22**(2):109-125. DOI: 10.1108/RJTA-08-2017-0041

[22] Gurarda A, Meric B. Slippage and grinning behavior of lockstitch seams in elastic fabrics under cyclic loading conditions. Textile and Apparel. 2010;**20**(1):65-69

[23] American Association of Textile Chemists & Colours - AATCC88B. Smoothness of Seams in Fabrics After Repeated Home Laundering. USA: American Association of Textile Chemists & Colours; 2018

[24] Hati S, Das BR. Seam pucker in apparels: A critical review of evaluation methods. Asian Journal of Textile. 2011;**1**(2):60-73. DOI: 103923/ajt.2011.60.73

[25] Sauri RM, Manich AM, Barella A, Loria J. A factorial study of seam resistance in woven and knitted fabrics. Textile Journal of Textile Research. 1987;**12**:188-193

[26] Stylios GK, Zhu R. The mechanism of sewing damage in knitted fabrics. Journal of the Textile Institute. 1998;**89**(2):411-421. Part-1

[27] Thilagavathi G, Viju S. Process control in apparel manufacturing. In: Majumdar A, Das A, Alagirusamy R, Kothari VK, editors. Process Control in Textile Manufacturing. UK: Woodhead Publishing; 2013. pp. 475-492. ISBN: 978-0-85709-027-0

[28] Dorkin CMC, Chamberlain NH. The facts about needle heating. Clothing Institution Technology Report; 1963. p. 63

[29] Kar J, Fan J, Yu W. Women's apparel: Knitted underwear. In: Au KF, editor. Advances in Knitted Technology. UK: Woodhead Publishing; 2011. pp. 235-261. DOI: 10.1533/9780857090621.3.235

[30] Gotlih K. Zunic-Lojen D. The relation between viscoelastic properties of the thread and sewing needle penetration force. In: The 78th World Conference of the Textile Institute in Association with the 5th Textile Symposium of SEVE and SEPVE, Greece; 1997. pp 133-147

Chapter 3

Innovation in the Comfort of Intimate Apparel

Abstract

Intimate apparel is the most important clothing layer since it acts as human's second skin due to contact with the skin directly. The comfort issues for intimate apparels are sensorial, thermal, motion, and aesthetical, all of which are interrelated. Since intimate apparel is an inner layer in between the skin and the outerwear, its thermal comfort is very important. Transferring moisture from the clothing to the environment through diffusion, wicking, sorption, and evaporation is regulated by the thickness and tightness of the fabric. On the other part, the behavior of fabric is affected by chemical and physical properties of its constituent fibers, fiber content, physical and mechanical characteristics of its constituent yarns, and the finishing treatments. Thus, major fiber manufacturers such as Nylstar, Invista, and Lenzing have launched different types of fibers such as Meryl Skinlife, Tactel, Tencel, etc., which are suitable for intimate apparel. The aim of this chapter is to introduce the latest developments in fibers used in the manufacturing of intimate apparel products and their contribution to clothing comfort, which the apparels give when the body does not limit its movement and regulation mechanism of its own temperature.

Keywords: intimate apparel, new fibers, thermal comfort, sensorial comfort, body movement comfort

1. Intimate apparel

Intimate apparel is a kind of garment which is worn next to the skin, and thus it behaves as human's second skin. Conventional bra, underwear, sports bra, pantyhose, swimwear, mastectomy bra as well as maternity underwear, body shaper, and corset are described as intimate apparel, and this kind of apparel is an interdisciplinary subject involving body beauty, human anatomy and anthropometrics, pattern design, textile engineering, as well as health science [1]. As intimate apparel contacts with the skin directly, its comfort characteristics are more important than that of outerwear, and from this point of view in this chapter, comfort performances of intimate apparels were discussed.

2. What is comfort?

Comfort is a complex state of mind that depends on many physical, physiological, and psychological factors [2]. Slater defined comfort as "a pleasant state of physiological, psychological and physical harmony between a human being and the environment" [3]. The impact of clothing on comfort and performance of individuals at work or sport is of particular importance because physiological loads may decline the physical and mental capacity of the person [4]. Also, various consumers consider comfort as one of the most important attributes in their purchase of apparel products; therefore companies tend to focus on the comfort of apparel products [2]. Intimate wear, which is described as human's second skin, requires the comfort issue to be maintained perpetually than that of outerwear due to the contact to the skin directly. Also, the daily performance and good feeling of a person are synonymous with intimate apparel comfort characteristics.

Wear comfort can be divided into four main aspects such as thermal comfort, sensorial comfort, body movement comfort, and aesthetic comfort. Thermal comfort is the satisfaction of a person with the thermal environment, and to do so there is a thermal balance between the human body and the environment and the proper balance between body heat production and heat loss. Thus, the person feels neither too cold nor too warm. In addition to heat transfer, moisture transport through the body-clothing-environment system is the main topic of the thermal comfort [2, 5]. Sensorial comfort refers to neural sensations when a fabric or garment comes into contact with human skin. It includes the warmth/coolness, prickliness, surface roughness, and electrical properties (e.g., static) of fabric against skin. Body movement comfort refers to the ability of a textile to allow freedom of movement [2]. Aesthetic comfort is the subjective perception by visual sensation which is influenced by color, style, garment fitting, fashion compatibility, fabric construction, and finish [1, 6].

2.1 Aesthetic comfort

Female consumers, regardless of age and social status, are concerned with keeping up with the fashion trends though fashion items such as laced bras and thongs may be less comfortable to wear than daily bras and basic underwear. Despite an inherent incapacity to display the product, consumers feel they want it to be relevant and fashionable [7]. Thus, intimate apparel is invisible to the public, but it is considered as "inconspicuous fashion" [8].

Bras allow the wearer to express their personality as they contribute to the final breast shape and contour visible through outer clothing that constructs a social identity [8]. Women may lose their youthful appearance after pregnancy, aging, or menopause. So, they would need a bra that makes the breasts look firm, round, and natural. The bra should uplift the drooping breasts to a desirable position with necessary fullness, coverage, and cleavage. On the other hand, the woman who has a plus size breast may suffer from social anxiety, low comfort level, and difficulty in their self-esteem, thinking that her outstanding breast causes shame [9]. Thus, many brands including Berlei, Victoria's Secret, Triumph, and Bonds carry a wide range of bras that provide suitable comfort, support, and fit according to the needs of growing teens, working women, nursing mothers, and older women. Brands have also distinguished between different bra-wearing behaviors by differentiating the product into usage patterns, such as occasions and benefits sought (e.g., T-shirt bra designed for seamless everyday wear, push-up bras for enhanced cleavage, convertible bras for strapless or halter neck outfits, and sports bra for physical activities) [10].

2.2 Thermal comfort

The main property of clothing is to build a stable microclimate next to the skin in order to maintain the body's thermoregulatory system at different environmental and physical activity conditions, and provision of thermal balance is a function of the clothing in all wear situations. It acts as a barrier to heat and vapor transfer between skin and environment. Thermal comfort depends on several factors, heat and vapor transport, sweat absorption, and drying ability [4, 11], and it is an important criterion for intimate apparel in terms of feeling comfortable. Intimate apparel, being an inner layer in between the skin and outerwear, should be capable of maintaining heat balance between the excess heat produced by the wearer and the capacity of the clothing to dissipate body heat and perspiration. However, it exists within a narrow temperature range [12].

Human body is homoeothermic and has to maintain its core temperature around 37°C, with a skin temperature between 30.7 and 35.6°C [13]. The body cells, especially in the organs and the muscles, produce heat that is partly released to the environment. This metabolic heat production can largely vary depending on the activity, from about 80 W at rest to over 1000 W during most strenuous efforts [2]. At an extreme activity, the heat produced in the muscles creates the greatest thermal stress. A large amount of this heat is often stored in the body resulting in an increase in body temperature [13, 14]. Then, the central nervous system gives indication to the hypothalamus of brain which controls the thermoregulation process. It sends signals to human organs, muscles, glands, and the nervous system. The excess heat is liberated to the outer environment by means of heat loss mechanism process [15]. Heat transfer continues until the two media are the same temperature and have reached equilibrium. The rate of the energy transferred depends on temperature difference and the degree of resistance between the two media [12]. Heat transfer from the body to the environment occurs in several ways [2, 13, 16]:

- Dry heat transfer conduction (heat transfer between two surfaces in contact with each other), convection (heat exchange between a surface and a surrounding fluid, e.g., air or water), and radiation (emission or absorption of electromagnetic waves)
- Evaporation of sweat
- Heat transfer by respiration

In order to maintain the thermoregulation of a human body, heat generation and heat loss should ideally be equal. This principle can be expressed in a heat balance equation (Eq. (1)) (in W or W/m^2) for the human body [2]:

$$M - W = E + R + C + K + S \tag{1}$$

where M is metabolic rate of the body, W is mechanical work, E is heat transfer by evaporation, R is heat transfer by radiation, C is heat transfer by convection, K is heat transfer by conduction, and S is heat storage.

The enclosed still air and external air movement are the major factors that affect the heat transfer through fabric, and it is influenced by fabric construction, thickness, and material [4]. Fibers in a fabric structure serve two main functions in providing thermal insulation. Firstly, they develop air spaces and prevent air movement. Secondly, they provide a shield to heat loss from radiation. The efficiency of the thermal insulation of a fabric depends on fiber physical properties, such as fineness and shape, as well as the structure of fabric [5]. The higher the volume of dead air within a textile structure, the lower will be the thermal transmittance which results in higher thermal resistance [15]; man-made fibers can be produced with a degree of crimp or surface irregularity that increases thermal resistance

[5]. Fabrics or garments made from hollow fibers can also provide better thermal insulation values due to the larger trapped air volume provided. Previous research shows that the amount of contact an item of clothing (such as a sports bra) has with the skin may affect thermoregulation. When the clothing fits tightly, there is less exchange of air beneath the clothing with the environment ("flushing"), and this can negatively affect thermoregulation [13]. Therefore, a sports bra, for example, can represent a physical advantage but a thermal disadvantage [13].

Evaporation is the body's main method of heat dissipation during exercise and in hot environments [13]. Heavy sweat is formed in the body that leads to the accumulation of a lot of moisture or a thin film on the skin due to heat dissipation [4]. Sweating majorly acts as a heat loss mechanism of the body and cools where the sweat is being evaporated. Clothing actively affects the amount of sweat produced and the level of evaporation [13]. When fabric is subjected to heavy sweating conditions, not all the sweat absorbed by fabric can be given off to the atmosphere instantaneously. Thus to prevent the wearer from feeling wet and clammy [17], the sweat should be transported away from the skin surface body. The transportation of sweat may be in the form of liquid or vapor so that the fabric touching the skin feels dry [11, 15].

In that respect, water vapor permeability is an important property that determines the capability of transporting perspiration through a textile material [15]. Water vapor permeability plays a very important role when there is only little sweating or insensible perspiration. The garment should have the ability to release the moisture vapor held in the microclimate to the atmosphere to reduce the dampness at the skin [4]. Impermeable structures, i.e., not permitting passage of water vapor to the surrounding atmosphere, increase the relative humidity of the microclimate inside the clothing and thermal conductivity of the insulating air, causing coolness and dampness. Water vapor transfer through textile materials may occur due to diffusion (driven by a water vapor concentration gradient) and convection (driven by an air pressure gradient) mechanisms [12]. Moisture transfer also involves adsorption, absorption, or desorption between the fibers and the surrounding air as well as the movement of condensed liquid water as a result of external forces, such as capillary pressure and gravity. Adsorption occurs when water molecules are attracted to the surface of a solid. A larger fiber surface area within a fabric can increase the amount of water adsorbed. In absorption, molecular moisture diffuses through the material. Desorption is the process of moisture release from adsorbed or absorbed water. The process of moisture absorption or desorption within textile materials absorbs or releases heat, which further complicates the heat transfer process [5]. The sweat absorption, spreading, and drying which determine how quickly the skin can be dried after sweating of a fabric decide the thermophysiological comfort property of the garment [18]. Therefore, fabrics with good moisture transport and drying properties are essential for intimate apparel which contact with skin directly.

During heavy activity when liquid perspiration production becomes high, to feel comfortable the clothing should possess good liquid transmission property. Wicking is an important property to uphold a feel of comfort during sweating conditions and is affected by fabric properties [4]. Discomfort is linked to the presence of liquid on the skin, and the removal of this, either by optimized evaporation or by wicking the moisture away from the skin, is thus a relevant factor [19]. Wicking is the spontaneous flow of liquid in a porous substrate, driven by capillary forces produced in the fabric. This is due to the wetting of fibers, and it causes the liquid to reach the spaces in between the fibers which gives a capillary action. Wicking fabrics can benefit comfort and cooling in two ways. When a person starts to sweat in garment, this sweat can be absorbed by fabric, spreading over a bigger area and thus facilitating evaporation. Also, by removing the liquid from the skin and transporting it away from the skin-fabric interface, clinging of clothing with its associated discomfort is reduced [4, 19]. The transport of liquid moisture is a complex mechanism dependent on the hydrophilic properties of the material (fibers), the inter- and intra-yarn capillaries, as well as the water absorption capacity (hygroscopicity) of fibers. These phenomena depend on the liquid surface tension, the size of the interstices, and wettability of fiber surface. The capillaries (interstices) in a fabric must form a continuous channel with the proper size. Parameters, such as fabric count, yarn linear density, and yarn twist, affect the size and number of fabric interstices. Fabrics with larger interstices normally allow rapid diffusion of water [20]. Sweat forming on the skin can be transported from the skin surface to the outer surface of the fabric by fabric wicking, where it evaporates to the environment and keeps the skin dry [5]. The spreading of liquid moisture can basically occur in two directions: spreading into the surface of the fabric (lateral wicking effect) or transfer of liquid from one side to the other (vertical wicking effect [2]). Also, moisture regain of a fiber affects wicking performance such that fiber with a larger moisture regain tends to decrease the wicking effect. In addition to these, the radius of capillaries is the key factor in deciding capillary effects [5].

Dryarn, Coolmax, FIELDSENSOR™, fibers from Meryl product line, AKWATEK, Moiscare™ fibers, and the others, which will be discussed in detail in following section, provide high thermal comfort performance.

2.3 Ease of movement comfort

People must be able to move in the clothing that they wear. If clothing restrains movement, discomfort may result due to the pressure exerted on the body by the garment, and the clothing may fail [21]. A simple and ordinary body movement expands the skin by about 10–50%. Therefore, the strenuous movements require the least resistance from garment and instant recovery [22]. The dramatic difference between the skin's elasticity and the lack of elasticity in conventional fabrics results in restriction of movement to the wearer and loss of shape, and consequent performance, of garments [9]. Minimizing a garment's resistance to the body's demands in movement can be achieved through increased fabric fullness in the pattern or through fabric stretch. Increasing the fabric's stretch means garments can be cut to achieve a more streamlined appearance and can conform better to the body while still maintaining comfort for the wearer in motion [21]. Thus, intimate apparel should have stretch and elastic recovery to provide sufficient fit and freedom of movement to the wearer.

Fitting is a crucial factor of wearing comfort particularly for the next-to-skin stretch garment. Despite attempts to standardize size, every female's body shape is unique, which complicates the design process [8]. A good bra should fit the 3D complex body contours, to support the breast weight and to provide appropriate tension by well-fitted bottom band, straps, and cups [23]. However, perfect fit for bras is very difficult to achieve because it involves tedious trials and errors on manipulating the shape and support provided to the soft breasts of a live model [9]. Moreover, many pattern adaptations may be required to try different grain lines in the pattern and tension of fabric or changing the fabric and trims for better tension recovery [24]. However, women go through great difficulties to find a perfect-fitting bra to mold the body in a desirable silhouette [9]. A research conducted across western countries reports that at least around 70% of women wears the wrong size of bras [23]. This is not surprising because even within the same brand the bra size and thus bra fit change with the different styles [24]. The big problem of wearing the wrong bra contributes to poor posture due to the lack of support for the chest, and muscles have to do all the breast work. The breast is pulled by weight bra and causes pain on the back, neck, and back pain [9]. According to a study, the ability of a sports bra is reduced due to the poor bra fit which causes an increased breast discomfort [24].

Creating irritation in skin areas, bruises, and deep creases on the skin by elastic pressing the wrong place make the user feel uncomfortable [9]. It was found that the highest pressure was at the top of the shoulders and under the front elastic band. Costantakos and Watkins [23] suggested that a well-designed bra should prevent concentration of pressure on the sensitive areas such as veins and arteries near the skin surface. To limit the force generation and increase breast comfort level, the positive correlation between the mass of the breast and the vertical displacement suffering in their day by day has to be found. Also, the plus size bra can be the cause of numerous health problems related to the arms, neck, back, and head pain. For a plus size bra, it is advisable to use powernet or more than 20% elastane or lining for the wing or band part. The percentage of elastane will increase support in plus size breast that can be improved with the placement of a bone on the lateral side fitting [9]. Moreover, in the particular stage of a woman's life, with the breast sagging, to create the right bra and the user choosing a more appropriate model, it is important to retain the biomechanical considerations. For pregnant women suffering from low back pain, maternity under garments could provide certain abdominal support and distribute the growing weight of fetus to the shoulder and the upper torso, which may help to relieve back pain and improve the wearer's mobility [23].

Garments including fibers such as LYCRA® W from the Lycra Company, the Meryl Elite® from Nylstar, and ISCRA-S from Sorona offer comfort in terms of fit, shape retention, and freedom of movement.

2.4 Sensorial comfort

Sensorial comfort is the sensation of how the fabric feels when it is worn near to the skin. The tribology of skin in contact with textiles is important in connection with the comfort of clothing, because the tactile properties of fabrics are closely related to their surface and frictional properties. Sensorial comfort is very difficult to predict as it involves a large number of different factors, and this feeling addresses properties of the fabric like prickling, itching, stiffness, or smoothness [2]. In addition, a good performance of movements is always combined with the use of suitable materials and intimate apparel; the proportion of the body has to be assessed so that the product used is the most appropriate for those wearing it [9]. In addition, wet skin is much more easily irritated than dry skin.

Experimental studies showed that raw materials and structural properties of fabrics are important in the determination of tactile properties of fabrics. Suda and Tamura [23] tried to estimate comfort with the help of the tactile sensations like smoothness, softness, and stickiness of underwear fabrics despite the change in air temperature. According to Nielsen et al. [25], knit structures of the underwear influenced sensations of humidity significantly, but not sensations of temperature. The various sensations of temperature correlated best with core temperature, whereas the sensations of humidity correlated with skin wetness. The study which assesses the tactile comfort according to 10 descriptors (soft, thin, smooth, warm, dry, light, loose, sheer, stiff, and pleasant tactile sensation) conducted by Kweon et al. [23] implied that men usually preferred all cotton, while women selected man-made fabrics. In addition, at intimate apparel lace and embroidery are used so often which prick the skin. Also, poor seam coverings or loose threads also bring skin irritation. To minimize the seams and stitches, various sew-free technologies have been widely applied. The bra cup seams have been eliminated by molded cups; the elastic band has been replaced by Bemis thermoplastic polyurethane (TPU) film or Lycra 2.0 polyurethaneurea (PUU) heat-activated elastic adhesive tape. Thread and stitches disappear when the hemming operation uses ultrasonic bonding with hooks and eyes integrally attached onto the inner surface of the back wing panel. Brand and size labels are seamlessly printed [23]. A study of 1285 female marathon runners found 28% frequently experienced problems with sports bras rubbing or chaffing which is a typical example of the importance of sensorial comfort which if ignored may lead to minor injuries [24]. Moreover, women have sensitive skin especially during puberty and pregnancy.

TACTEL® fiber from Invista, Sensil® Body Fresh, and chitin are some examples for the novel fibers that maintain good sensorial comfort.

3. Innovative fibers and comfort of intimate apparel

"A fiber is a unit of matter, either natural or manufactured, characterized by flexibility, fineness and a high ratio of length to thickness" [26]. The use of natural fibers dates back to 4000 years ago, and they were the fibers used first. Cotton, wool, silk, and all other animal and plant fibers fall in the category of natural fibers. The first attempt to make an artificial fiber was done in the year 1664. However, it was almost 200 years later when the first success was achieved. Man-made fibers became a significant alternative to natural fibers after the 1950s. The development of these fibers opened up fiber applications to various fields like medicine, agriculture, home furnishing, modern apparels, etc. [27, 28]. The timetable of fibers covers four generations [29]:

- Before the 1950s, natural fibers were used, and they are termed as first-generation fibers.
- After the 1950s, second-generation fibers, man-made regenerated and synthetic ones, were introduced.
- Third-generation fibers came in the 1980s. This generation covered specialty fibers, high-performance/high functional fibers, and high technology fibers.
- Super fibers, smart fibers, and nanofibers, which are called new fibers, are the fourth-generation fibers that came after 1985. These fibers give a new dimension to the use of textiles.

As of today, latest trends and innovations in man-made fiber and textile industry can be roughly identified and classified as follows [30]:

- Sustainability
- Development of functional textile
- Development of smart textile
- Manufacturing innovations
- Materials engineering
- Unconventional applications

High-technology fiber is a general term used for fibers made by different methods from ordinary methods, and they are the ones which have improved performance such as high melting point and high decomposition temperature. These high-function fibers are developed according to needs of the user and provide higher comfort, easy-care properties. Functional textiles have additional functionalities like flame resistance, breathability, thermoregulation, stain resistance, being antimicrobial, electro conductivity, etc. [31].

Common types of fibers currently used in intimate apparel are cotton, silk, rayon, nylon, polyester, and spandex. Performance and versatility of intimate apparel such as easy-care properties, light weight, durability, ease of movement, having antibacterial or anti-odor properties, and good moisture management are further improved by the use of new fibers. In this section the latest developments in fibers used in the manufacturing of intimate apparel products and their contribution to clothing comfort are discussed [32].

Fibers which attribute ease of movement to intimate garments have superior stretch and recovery properties:

LYCRA® is a synthetic elastane fiber that can stretch up to about six times its initial length and return to its original state repeatedly. Garments including LYCRA® fiber offer comfort, fit, shape retention, and freedom of movement. The fiber can be used in close-to-the-body garments such intimate apparel as well as pantyhose, hosiery, active wear, and swimwear [33].

LYCRA® W technology offered by the Lycra Company elevates the performance of intimate apparel made from warp or circular knit fabrics. "W" elastane fibers with luster permit the garments to deliver outstanding whiteness, whiteness retention, uniformity, and dye pickup for deeper, richer colors. Fabrics made with these fibers also have better resistance to elastane yellowing from heat-setting, exposure to fumes, and UV light [34].

For intimates, body wear, sportswear, etc., different types of polyamide microfibers are offered by Nylstar through the Meryl® product line.

Meryl Elite provides a convenient partnership to elastane in single and double covered yarns (**Figure 1**) offering a good performance for tights, socks, and leggings. Microfilaments of Meryl Elite give lightness, smoothness, high elasticity, durability, and comfort to the garments [35].

ISCRA-S is a highly elastic material-like spandex. It is a bicomponent fiber from Sorona, a material extracted from corn, and PET. After the finishing processes are applied, it gains a spring-like structure (**Figure 2**) [36].

The fiber is suitable to be used in underwear, sportswear, outdoor wear, etc. due to its comfort stretch and good stretch recovery as well as quick moisture absorbing and drying properties.

ECOWAY-Sorona from corn is a soft touch fiber from shape memory material recommended for intimate apparel. Textiles from ECOWAY-Sorona are naturally crumpled and smoothly unfolded due to the shape memory property [37].

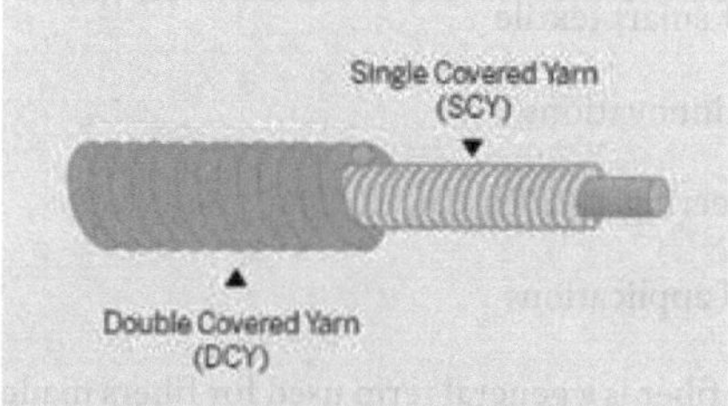

Figure 1.
Covered yarn structure [35].

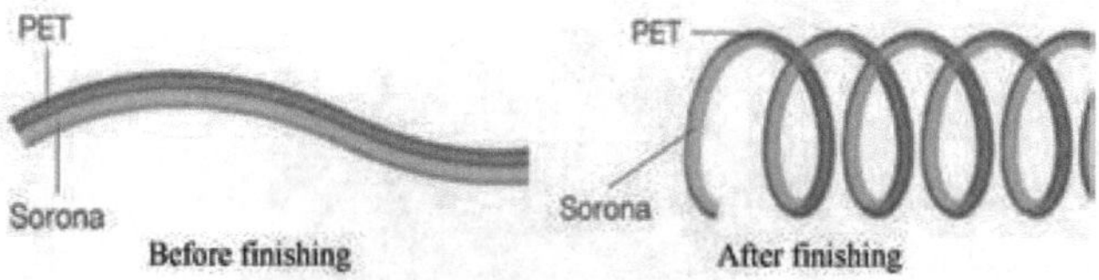

Figure 2.
ISCRA-S fiber before and after finishing process [36].

To improve moisture management properties of intimate apparel, breathable fibers with modified cross section have been developed to enhance the wearer's comfort. Fibers and yarns that possess improved moisture management properties are discussed in the following section:

TENCEL™ Intimate cellulosic fibers, lyocell, and modal are produced by sustainable processes from natural, renewable raw material, wood. TENCEL™ lyocell fibers absorb moisture more effectively than synthetic fibers, and there is less moisture formed on the fiber. The fibrils of cellulosic fibers regulate the absorption and release of moisture. This leads to less favorable media for bacterial growth, and consequently better hygienic qualities are offered. This also enhances breathability of the garment and keeps the skin cool and dry. One of the key factors in choosing materials for intimate apparel is softness. The smooth surface of TENCEL™ Intimate cellulosic fibers also offers a gentle touch to the skin. High flexibility and low rigidity of fine TENCEL Modal fibers result in a soft feeling twice as soft as cotton [38].

FIELDSENSOR™, developed by Toray, applies the principles of capillary transport to the structure of knitwear enabling absorption, movement, dispersion, and evaporation of perspiration from the skin. By this way, the perspiration-induced stickiness and clinginess of traditional materials are eliminated. It offers good moisture management functions for running, fitness, and training suits [39, 40].

Flat multi-microfibers as fine as 0.45 dpf (dtex per filament) of Meryl® Sublime, from Nylstar's Meryl® product line, quickly draw perspiration away from the skin to the exterior of the fabric. The fiber is highly demanded for intimates and swimwear due to its special handle, silky touch, light weight, and breathability [41].

Meryl® Nateo is an air-textured polyamide yarn with a round cross section. The main properties of Meryl Nateo, namely, UV productivity, water absorption, breathability, and stretch ability, make the fiber suitable to be used in body wear, sport, swimwear, or intimates [42].

Trilobal cross section of Meryl Satiné reflects the light perfectly and provides garments with a remarkable shine comparable to silk (**Figure 3**). Meryl Satiné is preferred for many applications due to its excellent moisture-wicking properties, breathability, and natural elasticity [43].

Dryarn is a breathable "isostatic polypropylene microfiber" which offers intense performance in terms of lightness, drying, and wicking, with no penalty in the thermal insulation properties specific to polypropylene. It also has a higher capacity for removing moisture compared to polyester [44, 45].

NILIT®, a manufacturer of nylon 6.6 fibers, offers fashion body wear, active wear, legwear, and intimate apparel. Sensil is a new Nylon 6.6 brand created by NILIT®. Sensil® Aquarius has built-in moisture management properties thanks to its special triple T-cross section which forms special micro-channels in the fiber and increases the surface area for improved moisture management (**Figure 4**) [46, 47].

Supplex®, a registered trademark of Invista and licensed by NILIT® for nylon fiber products, provides functional benefits for intimate apparel, active wear/fitness, etc. with an exceptionally smooth, natural hand due to the presence of finer,

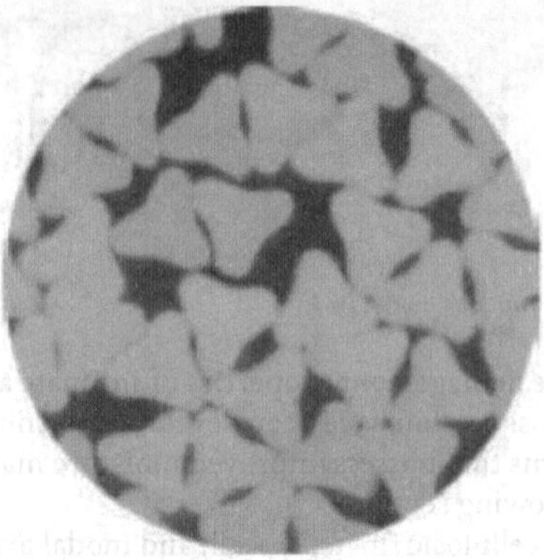

Figure 3.
Trilobal cross section of Meryl Satiné [43].

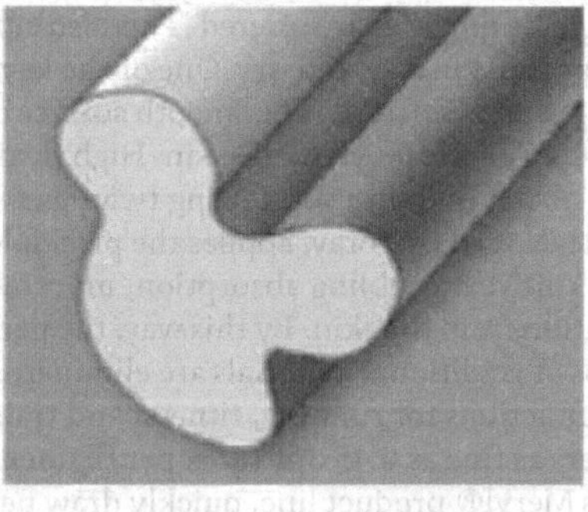

Figure 4.
T-cross section of Sensil® Aquarius [48].

multiple nylon filaments and dries up to four times faster than cotton. Supplex® also has permanent protection due to the intrinsic UPF protection qualities [49].

Coolmax is an advanced polyester yarn mainly used for thermoactive underwear, intimate apparel, sport underwear, and sportswear. A capillary transport system maintained by special four- or six-channeled fiber morphology pulls moisture away from the skin, transfers to the outer layer of the fabric, and dries quickly. It's much convenient for sport applications due to high thermal control under physical stress [50, 51].

Coolmax freshFX, on the other hand, is a suitable fiber for intimate apparel which combines the Coolmax® moisture management and odor shield antimicrobial fiber technologies. Coolmax® freshFX™ is designed by incorporating a silver-based additive to Coolmax. Coolmax® freshFX™ fabrics actively suppress the growth of bacteria which are responsible for body odor and related smells. Coolmax® freshFX™ garments keep the wearer cool and dry while keeping clothes smelling clean and fresh longer [52].

TACTEL® fiber from Invista is a form of nylon fiber which is widely used in women's intimate apparel because of its soft and lightweight nature, quick drying, easy care, breathability, and abrasion-resistant properties [53, 54].

Nike Dri-FIT technology uses microfibers to support the body's natural cooling system by wicking away sweat. The moistures is, then, dispersed evenly throughout the surface of the garment and evaporates quickly. Dri-FIT fabrics can be made of nylon, polyester, spandex, or a blend of all three but mostly in the form of microfibers. It is proposed that it should be worn next to the skin to keep the body dry [55].

Consumers' awareness of hygiene and active lifestyle has created an increasing demand for antimicrobial/anti-odor textiles. Bacteriostatic fabrics prevent the proliferation of microorganisms and production of unpleasant odor. The formation of fungal growth is also slowed down by the use novel fibers offered.

Normally, some amount of bacteria is present on human skin. Not only the presence of a high level of bacteria but also its complete absence creates various problems such as allergy, odor, illness, etc. While exercising, bacteria are transferred to the textile and with conventional nylon fibers; these bacteria can proliferate and grow very quickly. With the inherent silver microparticles, Meryl Skinlife prevents bacteria growth, maintains the natural balance of the skin, and reduces unpleasant odor [56].

Meryl Nexten from Nylstar is a hollow polyamide fiber with inherent silver microparticles (**Figure 5**). Its hollow structure provides the production of 20% lighter fabrics with the same thickness and insulation of the body against temperature variations. The presence of silver microparticle Meryl Nexten offers an antimicrobial effect [57].

Chitin is a biocompatible compound obtained from the shell of crab and shellfish. Chitosan is a product derived from Chitin. A new fiber Crabyon® is a blend of chitosan and viscose which has permanent antibacterial functions. The fiber is suitable for weak and sensitive skin since it prevents the skin from drying out. Due to Crabyon's velvety touch and other properties, it is recommended to be used in intimate apparel [58].

Sensil® Body Fresh makes sure the garments do not have unpleasant odor thanks to the antibacterial additive embedded in the fiber [59].

With its excellent disinfection power due to the silver ions held in the acrylic fibers, PURECELL™ and a deodorizing fiber preventing unpleasant smell by absorbing the ammonia CELFINEN™ are fibers recommended for underwear by TOYOBO [60, 61].

X-STATIC® silver fiber from Noble Fiber Technologies also utilizes the power of silver to inhibit the growth of bacteria on fabrics and to eliminate human-based odor. 99.9% metallic silver is bonded to the surface of a fiber X-STATIC® permanently. One hundred percent coverage area of silver on the fiber gives products with X-STATIC® a maximized performance with soft, flexible, and comfortable features [62].

TruFresh from Unifi is recommended for yoga pants, socks, hosiery, etc., for its odor-killing performance by inhibiting the growth of odor-causing bacteria, mold,

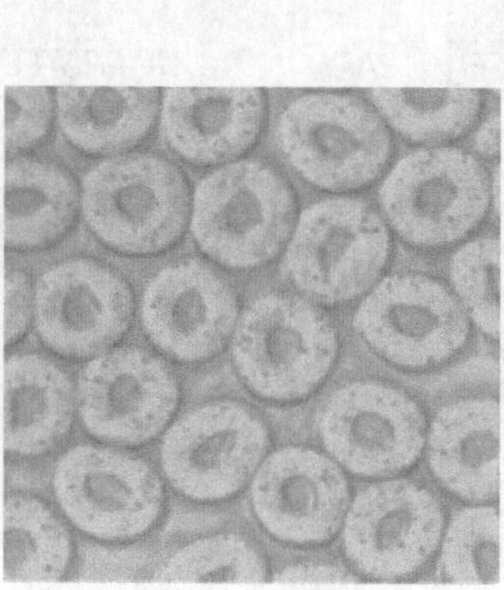

Figure 5.
Hollow polyamide fiber Meryl Nexten from Nylstar [57].

mildew, and algae on fabrics. For optimal performance, it is recommended that the fabric contains at least 30% TruFresh by weight [63].

Thermal comfort is related to the efficiency of heat dissipation from a clothed human body. One of the primary functions of underwear is to act as a buffer against environmental changes to maintain a thermal balance between the body heat and the heat lost to the environment while allowing the skin to remain free of liquid water. Thermal comfort is provided by the use of recently developed fibers [1].

AKWATEK is a modified polyester fiber with active surface layer with anionic end groups. The active surface transports water molecules and releases them to the atmosphere before they can form liquid water. Thanks to AKWATEK's enhanced properties, thermoregulatory actions of the body are duplicated, and moisture is pulled away from the body much faster than capillary action fabrics. AKWATEK has the ability of keeping the wearer cool in warm temperatures and warm in cold temperatures. It is used in fabrics with Lycra—for apparel tops and tank tops, sport bras, turtlenecks, tights, and leggings [23, 64].

Quick transfer of heat from the body is maintained by the wide surface area of the fiber with flat cross section, and comfort is enhanced by the cooling effect and efficient ventilation of Sensil® Breeze (**Figure 6**). The presence of inorganic micron particles in the polymer further increases the surface area and contributes to the cooling effect [65].

The use of Sensil® Heat in knitted garments provides a delay in heat transfer from the body to the outside. Coffee charcoal, from coffee bean shell residue, is integrated in the yarn together with an oxide additive which captures and keeps body heat. It is claimed that the insulation activity is most effective when the fabric is used nearest to the body [65].

Another fiber recommended for underwear, sports apparel, bed clothes, etc. is an acrylate fiber, Moiscare™, which is a registered trademark of the Japanese firm TOYOBO. The fiber has heat-generating ability when absorbing moisture. It is claimed that the exothermic energy is about three times higher than that of wool. Depending on the atmospheric conditions, it can absorb and release moisture repeatedly. It also has the ability of deodorizing ammonium gas and others [67].

Thermolite FIR technology from Invista is a spun-dyed black fiber in which special ceramic pigments are embedded. The fiber, recommended for legwear, absorbs the wearer's infrared radiation and reflects it back as heat energy and raises skin temperature by around 1°C [68].

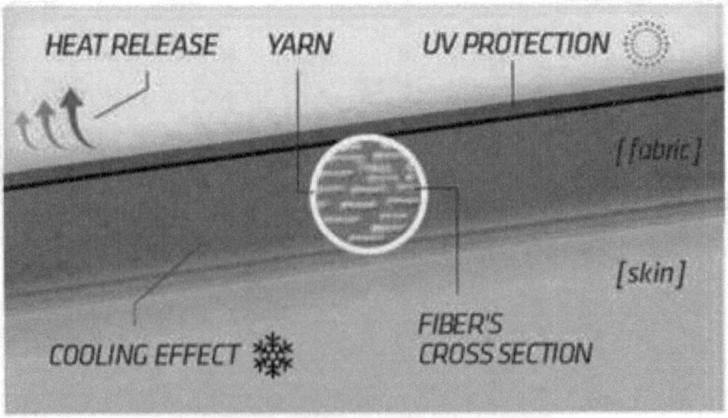

Figure 6.
Sensil® Breeze [66].

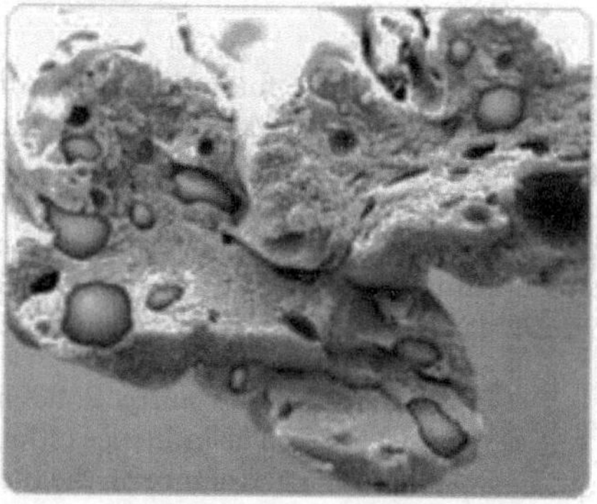

Figure 7.
Outlast® viscose fiber [70].

Outlast® technology manages moisture by reacting to sweat and pulling it away from the skin and proactively manages heat while controlling the production of moisture before it begins. It utilizes phase change materials (PCM) that absorb, store, and release heat for optimal thermal comfort. Outlast® phase change materials can be located inside the fiber. In-fiber applications are for products being worn next to or very close to the skin. Outlast® viscose is a versatile fiber commonly used for underwear, shirts, dresses, sleepwear, work wear, and sportswear (**Figure 7**). The fiber provides softness and comfort similar to cotton or silk [69, 70].

4. Conclusion

Intimate apparel ensures primarily the comfort of people as it contacts with the skin directly and forms an inner layer between the skin and outerwear. To provide intimate apparel comfort, thermal, aesthetical, sensorial, hygienic, and motional performances are required which are mostly related to fiber properties. Thus, the investigations to develop new fibers which provide better comfort performances are carried on by major fiber manufacturers. This chapter presents a detailed review of comfort from intimate apparel side, and also developed novel fibers which are recommended to be used for performing intimate apparel comfort were introduced.

References

[1] Kar J, Fan J, Yu W. Performance evaluation of knitted underwear. In: Yu W, Fan J, Harlock SC, Ng SP, editors. Innovation and Technology Of Women's Intimate Apparel. 1st ed. Cambridge: Woodhead Publishing Limited; 2006. pp. 196-222. ISBN-13: 978-1-84569-169-1

[2] Rossi R. Comfort and thermoregulatory requirements in cold weather clothing. In: Williams JT, editor. Textiles for Cold Weather Apparel. 1st ed. Oxford: Woodhead Publishing Limited; 2009. pp. 3-18. ISBN: 978-1-84569-717-4

[3] Wu HY, Zhang WY, Li J. Study on improving the thermal-wet comfort of clothing during exercise with an assembly of fabrics. Fibers & Textiles in Eastern Europe. 2009;**17**(4):46-51

[4] Suganthi T, Senthilkumar P. Thermo-physiological comfort of layered knitted fabrics for sportswear. Tekstil ve Konfeksiyon. 2017;**27**(4):352-360

[5] Song G. Thermal insulation properties of textiles and clothing. In: Williams JT, editor. Textiles for Cold Weather Apparel. 1st ed. Oxford: Woodhead Publishing Limited; 2009. pp. 19-32. ISBN: 978-1-84569-717-4

[6] Li Y. The science of clothing comfort. Textile Progress. 2001;**31**:1-2

[7] Granot E, Greene H, Brashear TG. Female consumers: Decision-making in brand-driven retail. Journal of Business Research. 2010;**63**:801-808

[8] Tsarenko Y, Strizhakova Y. "What does a woman want?" The moderating effect of age in female consumption. Journal of Retailing and Consumer Services. 2015;**26**:41-46

[9] Filipe AB, Carvalho C, Montagna G, Freire J. The fitting of plus size bra for middle aged women. Procedia Manufacturing. 2015;**3**:6393-6399

[10] Tsarenko Y, Lo CJ. A portrait of intimate apparel female shoppers: A segmentation study. Australasian Marketing Journal. 2017;**25**:67-75

[11] Onofrei E, Rocha AM, Catarino A. The influence of knitted fabrics' structure on the thermal and moisture management properties. Journal of Engineered Fibers and Fabrics. 2011;**6**(4):10-22

[12] Kaplan S, Okur A. A new dynamic sweating hotplate system for steady-state and dynamic thermal comfort measurements. Measurement Science and Technology. 2010;**21**(8):1-8

[13] Ayres B, White J, Hedger W, Scurr J. Female upper body and breast skin temperature and thermal comfort following exercise. Ergonomics. 2013;**56**(7):1194-1202

[14] Mijovic B, Skenderi Z, Salopek I. Comparison of subjective and objective measurement of sweat transfer rate. Collegium Antropologicum. 2009;**33**:509-514

[15] Suganthi T, Senthilkumar P. Development of tri-layer knitted fabrics for shuttle badminton players. Journal of Industrial Textiles. 2018;**48**(4):738-760

[16] Manshahia M, Das A. Comfort characteristics of knitted active sportswear: Heat and mass transfer. Research Journal of Textile and Apparel. 2013;**17**(3):50-60

[17] Suganthi T, Senthilkumar P, Dipika V. Thermal comfort properties of a bi-layer knitted fabric structure for volleyball sportswear. Fibers & Textiles in Eastern Europe. 2017;**25**(1):75-80

[18] Chen Q, Maggie TKP, Ma P, Jiang G, Xu C. Thermophysiological

comfort properties of polyester weft-knitted fabrics for sports T-shirt. The Journal of the Textile Institute. 2017;**108**(8):1421-1429

[19] Havenith G. Laboratory assessment of cold weather clothing. In: Williams JT, editor. Textiles for Cold Weather Apparel. 1st ed. Oxford: Woodhead Publishing Limited; 2009. pp. 217-243. ISBN: 978-1-84569-717-4

[20] Kissa E. Wetting and wicking. Textile Research Journal. 1996;**66**(10):660-668

[21] Voyce J, Dafniotis P, Towlson S. Elastic textiles. In: Shishoo R, editor. Textiles in Sport. 1st ed. Woodhead Publishing Limited; 2005. pp. 204-230. ISBN-13: 978-1-84569-088-5

[22] Senthilkumar M, Anbumani N. Dynamics of elastic knitted fabrics for sportswear. Journal of Industrial Textiles. 2011;**41**(1):13-24

[23] Yu W. Achieving comfort in intimate apparel. In: Song G, editor. Improving Comfort in Clothing. 1st ed. Oxford: Woodhead Publishing Limited; 2011. pp. 427-448. ISBN 978-0-85709-064-5

[24] Whittingham L. Biomechanical assessment of sports bra performance [thesis]. Loughborough, United Kingdom: Loughborough University; 2016

[25] Nielsen R, Endrusick TL. Sensations of temperature and humidity during alternative work/rest and the influence of underwear knit structure. Ergonomics. 1990;**33**(2):221-234

[26] Denton MJ, Daniels PN. Textile Terms and Definitions. Manchester: The Textile Institute; 1963. p. 63

[27] History of Fiber Development. [Internet]. Available from: https://technicaltextile.net/articles/history-of-fiber-development-2442 [Accessed: 18-04-2019]

[28] Man Made Fiber. Available from: https://docplayer.net/23883182-Industrievereinigung-chemiefaser-e-v-man-made-fibers-the-way-from-production-to-use.html

[29] Sreenivasa HV. Introduction to Textile Fibers. 1st ed. Murthy Edition. New Delhi: Woodhead Publishing India; 1970

[30] Olesya S. Trends in made-made fiber and textile industry textile [thesis]. Politecnico di Milano; 2013

[31] Hongu T, Phillips GO, Takigami M. New Millenium Fibers. Cambridge: Woodhead Publishing; 2005

[32] Yip J. Advanced textiles for intimate apparel. In: Yu W, editor. Advances in Women's Intimate Apparel Technology. 1st ed. Cambridge: Woodhead Publishing; 2016. pp. 3-23. ISBN: 978-1-78242-390-4

[33] Lycra. [Internet]. Available from: https://www.lycra.com/en/ [Accessed: 18-04-2019]

[34] LYCRA® W. [Internet]. Available from: https://connect.lycra.com/en/Technologies-and-Innovations/Fiber-Technologies/W [Accessed: 18-04-2019]

[35] Meryl Elite. [Internet]. Available from: http://www.nylstar.com/brochures/Nylstar_Meryl_Elite_2014.pdf [Accessed: 18-04-2019]

[36] ISCRA-S. [Internet]. Available from: https://www.toray-tck.com/eng/product/product01.asp?idx=107 [Accessed: 18-04-2019]

[37] ECOWAY-Sorona. [Internet]. Available from: https://www.toray-tck.com/eng/product/product01.asp?idx=103

[38] TENCEL™. [Internet]. Available from: https://www.tencel.com/intimate [Accessed: 18-04-2019]

[39] Özdil N, Anand S. Recent developments in textile materials and products used for activewear and sportswear. Electronic Journal of Textile Technologies. 2014;8(3):68-83

[40] FIELDSENSOR. [Internet]. Available from: https://www.toray.com/products/textiles/tex_0060.html [Accessed: 18-04-2019]

[41] Meryl® Sublime. [Internet]. Available from: http://www.nylstar.com/brochures/Nylstar_Meryl_Sublime_2014.pdf [Accessed: 18-04-2019]

[42] Meryl® Nateo. [Internet]. Available from: http://www.nylstar.com/shops/yarns/244-meryl-nateo [Accessed: 18-04-2019]

[43] Meryl Satiné. [Internet]. Available from: http://www.nylstar.com/shops/yarns/256-meryl-satine [Accessed: 18-04-2019]

[44] Dryarn. [Internet]. Available from: https://www.aquafil.com/products/dryarn/# [Accessed: 18-04-2019]

[45] Lim NY, Yu W, Fan J, Yip J. Innovation of girdles. In: Yu W, Fan J, Harlock SC, Ng SP, editors. Innovation and Technology of Women's Intimate Apparel. 1st ed. Cambridge: Woodhead Publishing Limited; 2006. pp. 114-131. ISBN-13: 978-1-84569-169-1

[46] Sensil® Aquarius. [Internet]. Available from: http://www.sensil.com/ [Accessed: 18-04-2019]

[47] Sensil® Aquarius. [Internet]. Available from: http://www.nilit.com/fibers/products.asp [Accessed: 18-04-2019]

[48] Sensil® Aquarius. [Internet]. Available from: http://www.nilit.com/fibers/AppFiles/Brochures/Aquarius.pdf [Accessed: 18-04-2019]

[49] SUPPLEX®. [Internet]. Available from: http://www.nilit.com/fibers/brands-supplex.asp [Accessed: 18-04-2019]

[50] Coolmax. [Internet]. Available from: https://www.janmarsport.eu/en/coolmax [Accessed: 18-04-2019]

[51] Coolmax. [Internet]. Available from: http://coolmax.com/en/Technologies-and-Innovations/COOLMAX-PRO-technologies/ [Accessed: 18-04-2019]

[52] Coolmax Fresh FX. [Internet]. Available from: https://www.galjoen.nl/downloads/coolmax_freshfx_200.pdf [Accessed: 18-04-2019]

[53] TACTEL®. [Internet] Available from: https://itextiles.com.pk/tactel-fiber/ [Accessed: 18-04-2019]

[54] TACTEL®. [Internet] Available from: https://prezi.com/i0pddh_swncl/tactel-by-invista/ [Accessed: 18-04-2019]

[55] Dri-FIT. [Internet]. Available from: https://www.nike.com/gb/help/a/nike-dri-fit [Accessed: 18-04-2019]

[56] Meryl Skinlife. [Internet]. Available from: http://www.nylstar.com/shops/yarns/250-meryl-skinlife [Accessed: 18-04-2019]

[57] Meryl Nexten. [Internet]. Available from: http://www.nylstar.com/shops/yarns/258-meryl-nexten [Accessed: 18-04-2019]

[58] Crabyon®. [Internet]. Available from: https://www.swicofil.com/commerce/brands/various/crabyon [Accessed: 18-04-2019]

[59] Sensil® Body Fresh. [Internet]. Available from: http://www.sensil.com/

AppFiles/Sensil_Product_Brochure.pdf [Accessed: 18-04-2019]

[60] CELFINENTM. [Internet]. Available from: https://www.exlan.co.jp/wordpress/wp-content/uploads/2018/09/celfinen_jp_en.pdf [Accessed: 18-04-2019]

[61] PURECELL™. [Internet]. Available from: https://www.exlan.co.jp/wordpress/wp-content/uploads/2018/09/purecell_jp_en.pdf [Accessed: 18-04-2019]

[62] X-STATIC®. [Internet]. Available from: http://noblebiomaterials.com/xstatic-textiles/what-x-static/

[63] TruFresh. [Internet]. Available from: https://unifi.com/innovations/trufresh [Accessed: 18-04-2019]

[64] AKWATEK. [Internet]. Available from: http://www.krystalartfield.com/Akwatek/Akwatek.html [Accessed: 18-04-2019]

[65] Sensil® Heat. [Internet]. Available from: http://www.sensil.com/AppFiles/Sensil_Product_Brochure.pdf [Accessed: 18-04-2019]

[66] Sensil® Breeze. [Internet]. Available from: http://www.nilit.com/fibers/AppFiles/Brochures/Breeze.pdf [Accessed: 18-04-2019]

[67] TOYOBO. [Internet]. Available from: https://www.exlan.co.jp/wordpress/wp-content/uploads/2018/09/moiscare_jp_en.pdf [Accessed: 18-04-2019]

[68] Thermolite FIR. [Internet]. Available from: https://www.knittingindustry.com/lycra-unveils-new-technologies-at-annual-event/ [Accessed: 18-04-2019]

[69] Outlast®. [Internet]. Available from: http://www.outlast.com/en/technology/ [Accessed: 18-04-2019]

[70] Outlast®. [Internet]. Available from: http://www.outlast.com/en/applications/fiber/ [Accessed: 18-04-2019]

Section 2

Yarn Manufacturing

Chapter 4

Simulations of Yarn Unwinding from Packages

Abstract

Yarn unwinding from stationary packages has an important role in many textile processes. In order to achieve high unwinding velocity that can lead to increased production rate, it is necessary to develop packages with a suitable geometry, dimensions, and winding type. The optimal design of the package leads to an optimal form of the balloon and low and uniform tension at high unwinding speed. In this work I will show a simple mathematical model which can be used for simulating the unwinding process. Using experimental values I will find a relation between the angular velocity of the yarn around the axis and the tension. This will allow me to calculate the oscillations of the tension in the yarn during the unwinding from packages of different geometries and with different winding angles. I will find an optimal design for a package of a new generation.

Keywords: yarn unwinding, packages, parallel wounding, cross wounding, unwinding simulations, oscillations of the tension in yarn

1. Introduction

At the end of the production process of a spinning factory, yarn is wound on packages. Therefore, packages are a crucial intermediate product of textile industry. The rapid development of fast-running weaving and knitting machines has led to the situation where unwinding yarn from packages is one of the main production bottlenecks. For this reason it is of utmost importance to determine the package geometry and the winding angle which allow to maximize the unwinding velocity given the allowed highest yarn tension [1–6].

The yarn is being withdrawn with velocity V through an eyelet, where we also fix the origin O of our coordinate system (**Figure 1**). The yarn is rotating around the z axis with an angular velocity ω. At the lift-off point (Lp), the yarn lifts from the package and forms a balloon (the name stems from the fact that in one period of rotation, this part of the yarn describes a surface of evolution that has a form of a balloon). At the unwinding point (Up), the yarn starts to slide on the surface of the package. Angle ϕ is the winding angle of the yarn on the package. In order to be able to compare various package designs, it is necessary to determine the influence of the winding angle of the package on the angular velocity of the yarn forming the balloon, since the angular velocity determines to a great extend the yarn tensions. The results of simulations will be used to suggest a design for packages of new generations, on which two kinds of layers would alternate: parallel-wound layers and layers with high unwinding angle.

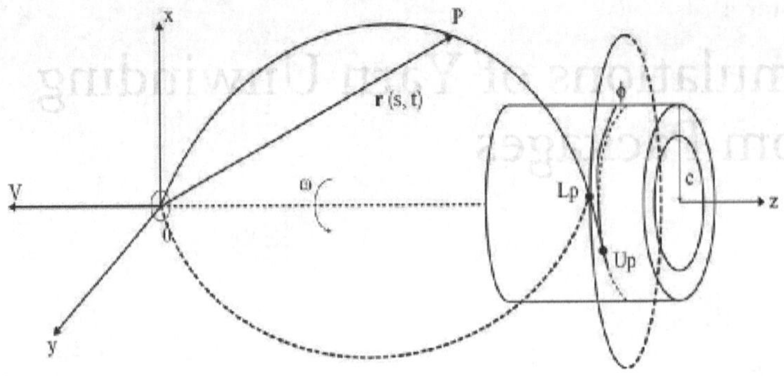

Figure 1.
Yarn unwinding from a cylindrical package.

2. Machines and materials

The current angular velocity ω for cylindrical packages is computed by using the relation [2, 3]

$$\omega = \frac{2\pi}{t} = \frac{V}{c}\frac{\cos\phi}{(1-\sin\phi)}. \tag{1}$$

In order to perform simulations, we additionally need a relation between the unwinding velocity and the yarn tension. The tension is largest in the eyelet through which the yarn is being pulled [3].

We measured tension for parallel-wound cylindrical packages of different dimensions and for different unwinding velocities (**Table 1**). For such packages the winding angle is $\phi \sim 0°$, and we obtain $\omega = V/c$. This is the expected result since in this case the unwinding velocity V equals the circumferential velocity of the lift-off point, which is given by $c\omega$ [3]. **Figure 2** shows the unwinding yarn system. Yarn is withdrawn from a fixed packages by a Lesson yarn drive at transport speed of up to 2000 m per minute. Support for the guide is fixed to which the sensor for measuring the tension of the yarn is installed.

Parameters	**Range of values**
Yarn type	Cotton
Yarn linear density *m*	0.8 g/m
Yarn titer *tex*	41.6 tex
Package radius *c*	92–110 mm
Package winding angle ϕ_0	5°
Package height *mm*	250 mm
Transport speed *V*	1000–2000 m/min

Table 1.
Experimental parameters.

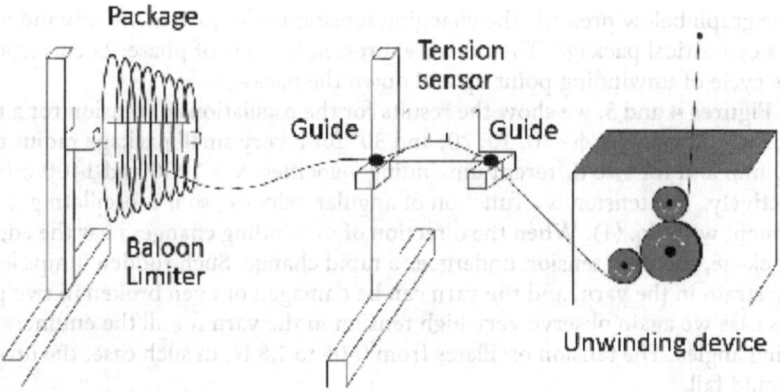

Figure 2.
Setup of the unwinding system.

3. Methods and simulation

In a recent paper, we developed a mathematical model [7, 8]:

$$f(t) = \text{sign}(\sin t)|\sin t|^{\frac{1}{40}} \tag{2}$$

which would permit to simulate the process of unwinding (**Figure 3**).
In our simulation we calculate the winding angle using the function

$$\phi_0(t) = \phi f(t) \tag{3}$$

where ϕ is the maximal angle of wind, then we determine the corresponding angular velocity ω, and finally we obtain an approximation for the tension using data from Section 2. In our calculations we considered unwinding for two consecutive layers of yarn, so that the package radius remains approximately constant during this time.

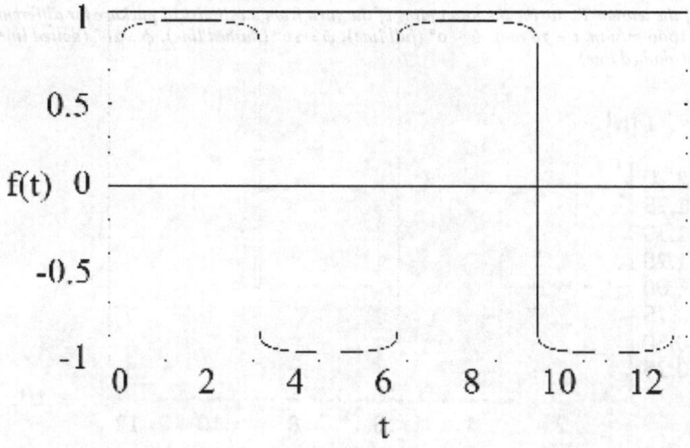

Figure 3.
Model function for winding angle.

The graph below presents the changing tension in the yarn as we unwind yarn from a cylindrical package. The time is expressed in units of phase: 2π corresponds to one cycle of unwinding point up and down the package.

In **Figures 4** and 5, we show the results for the oscillations of tension for a range of four winding angles $\phi \sim 0$, 10, 20, and 30° for a very small package radius of c = 70 mm and for two different unwinding velocities, V = 1000 and 1400 m/min, respectively. The tension is a function of angular velocity, so it is oscillating in agreement with Eq. (1). When the direction of unwinding changes near the edges of the package, the yarn tension undergoes a rapid change. Such sudden jumps lead to strong strain in the yarn, and the yarn can be damaged or even broken in two parts. In this case we again observe very high tension in the yarn for all the enumerated winding angles. The tension oscillates from 0.05 to 1.8 N. In such case, the unwinding would fail.

Figure 6 shows the time dependence of the yarn tension for unwinding velocity of V = 2000 m/min. The winding angle is fixed at $\varphi_0 = 5°$, and we consider package radii in the range from c = 70 to 500 mm. For large package radius, the tension is small, but it becomes sizable already at rather low radius between c = 100 and 200 mm. Nevertheless, the highest calculated tensions remain rather low, $T_0 = 0.7$ and 1.4 N.

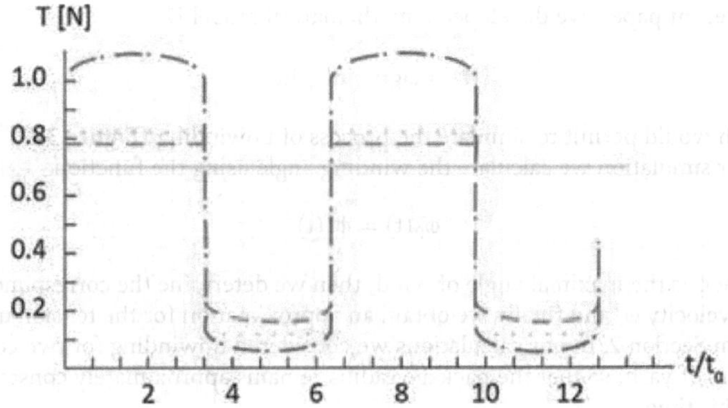

Figure 4.
Variation of the tension T_o during the unwinding of the yarn from a cylindrical package for different winding angles. V = 1000 m/min, c = 70 mm. $\phi \sim 0°$ (full line), $\phi = 10°$ (dashed line), $\phi = 20°$ (dotted line), and $\phi = 30°$ (dot-dashed line).

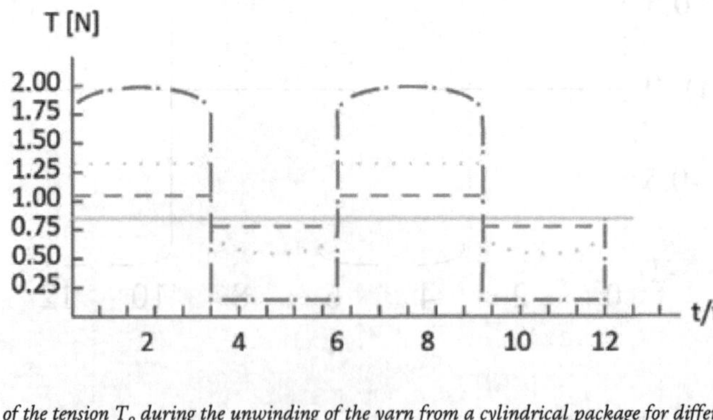

Figure 5.
Variation of the tension T_o during the unwinding of the yarn from a cylindrical package for different winding angles. V = 1400 m/min, c = 70 mm. $\phi \sim 0°$ (full line), $\phi = 10°$ (dashed line), $\phi = 20°$ (dotted line), and $\phi = 30°$ (dot-dashed line).

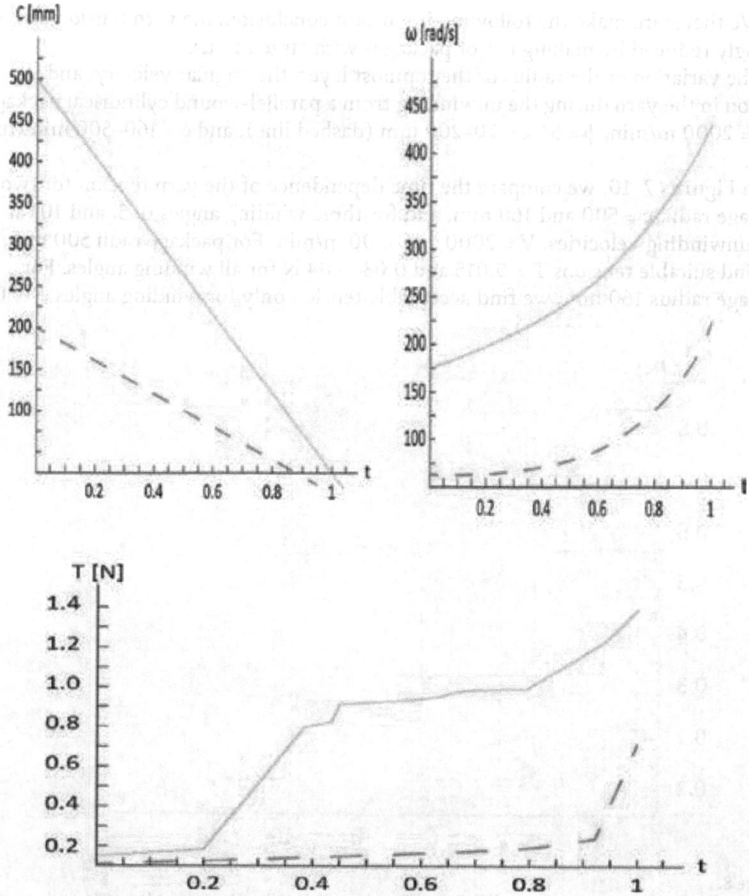

Figure 6.
Variation of the parameters during the unwinding from a package at V = 2000 m/min

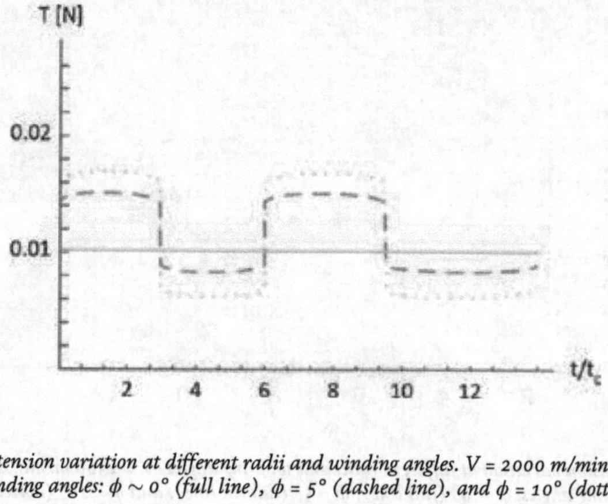

Figure 7.
Comparison of the tension variation at different radii and winding angles. V = 2000 m/min. The package radii is c = 500 mm. Winding angles: $\phi \sim 0°$ (full line), $\phi = 5°$ (dashed line), and $\phi = 10°$ (dotted line).

We therefore make the following important conclusion: the yarn tension can be strongly reduced by making use of packages with large radius.

The variation of the radius of the topmost layer, the angular velocity, and the tension in the yarn during the unwinding from a parallel-wound cylindrical package at V = 2000 m/min, $\phi = 5°$, c = 70–200 mm (dashed line), and c = 160–500 mm (full line).

In **Figures 7–10**, we compare the time dependence of the yarn tension for two package radii, c = 500 and 160 mm, and for three winding angles 0, 5, and 10° at two unwinding velocities, V = 2000 and 1500 m/min. For package radii 500 mm, we find suitable tensions T = 0.015 and 0.03–0.04 N for all winding angles. For package radius 160 mm, we find acceptable tension only for winding angles $\phi \sim 0$

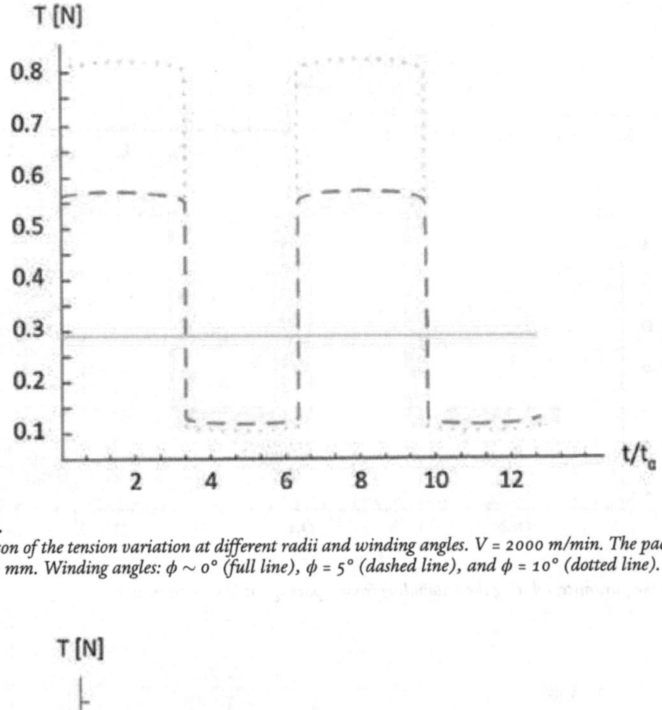

Figure 8.
Comparison of the tension variation at different radii and winding angles. V = 2000 m/min. The package radii is c = 160 mm. Winding angles: $\phi \sim 0°$ (full line), $\phi = 5°$ (dashed line), and $\phi = 10°$ (dotted line).

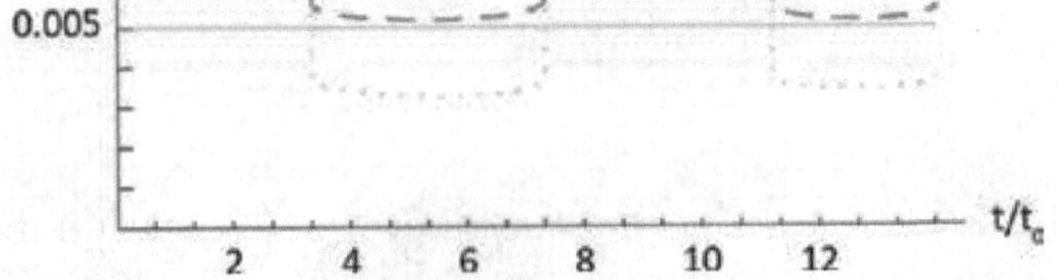

Figure 9.
Comparison of the tension variation at different radii and winding angles. V = 1500 m/min. The package radii is c = 500 mm. Winding angles: $\phi \sim 0°$ (full line), $\phi = 5°$ (dashed line), and $\phi = 10°$ (dotted line).

and ϕ = 5°: in these cases the tension rises at most to 0.055 N, which is at the higher end of the acceptable values. At ϕ = 10° we observe tensions around 0.08 N, which exceeds the limit.

Figures 11–13 show the dependence of the amplitude of tension oscillations as a function of the package radius (from 70 to 500 mm) and winding angle (from 0 to 20°) for three different unwinding velocities: 1000, 1500, and 2000 m/min. For all unwinding velocities, the oscillation amplitudes are larger for packages with smaller radius and large winding angle. In particular, the oscillations are very large for radii lower than 160 mm and for winding angles exceeding 5°.

The oscillations of yarn tension are related to the variation of the angular velocity of yarn rotation around the package axis.

The amplitude of the angular velocity oscillation is

$$\Delta\omega = \omega_{max} - \omega_{min} = \frac{2V}{c}\tan\phi \tag{4}$$

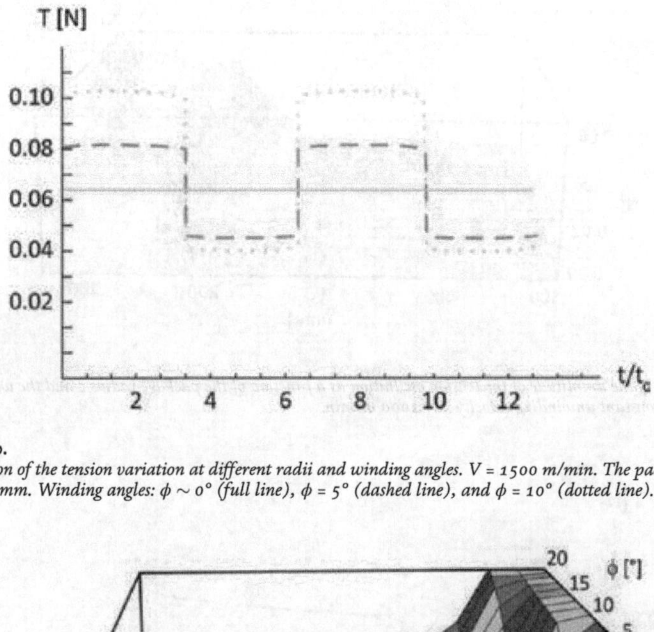

Figure 10.
Comparison of the tension variation at different radii and winding angles. V = 1500 m/min. The package radii is c = 160 mm. Winding angles: ϕ ~ 0° (full line), ϕ = 5° (dashed line), and ϕ = 10° (dotted line).

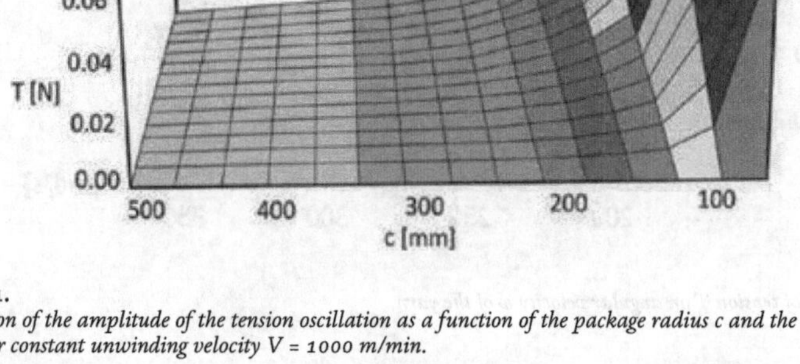

Figure 11.
Comparison of the amplitude of the tension oscillation as a function of the package radius c and the winding angle ϕ for constant unwinding velocity V = 1000 m/min.

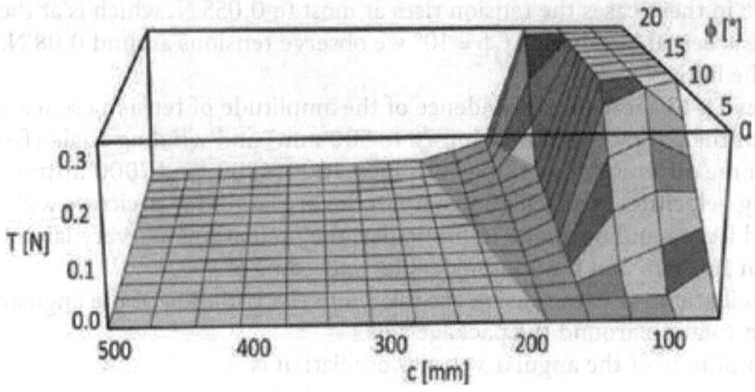

Figure 12.
Comparison of the amplitude of the tension oscillation as a function of the package radius c and the winding angle ϕ for constant unwinding velocity V = 1500 m/min.

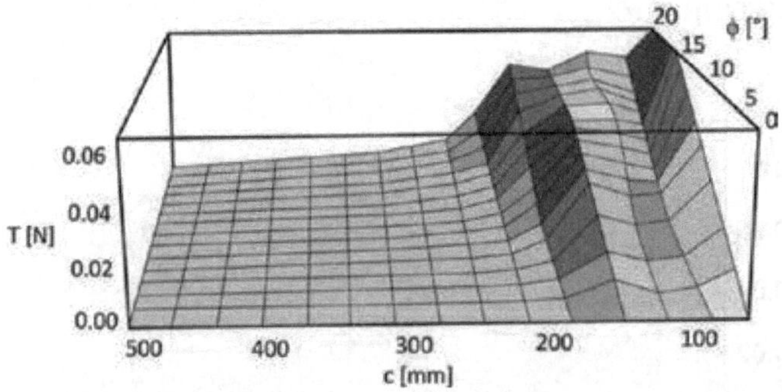

Figure 13.
Comparison of the amplitude of the tension oscillation as a function of the package radius c and the winding angle ϕ for constant unwinding velocity V = 2000 m/min.

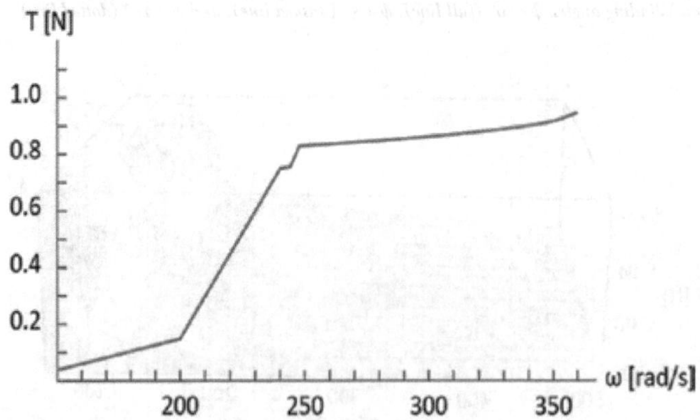

Figure 14.
Dependence of tension T on angular velocity ω of the yarn.

In the region of interest, i.e. for $\phi < 25°$, we have $\tan \phi \sim \phi$.
We get

$$\Delta\omega \approx \frac{2V\phi}{c}. \tag{5}$$

This means that the amplitude of the angular velocity oscillation is approximately proportional to the unwinding velocity and winding angle, but inversely proportional to the package radius.

From this relation we can estimate the yarn tension oscillation, knowing the dependence between the angular velocity and the tension that can be experimentally measured. We can also make use of **Figure 14**, which can serve to roughly estimate the amplitude of oscillations. We determine the average angular velocity during unwinding through

$$\omega_0 = \frac{(\omega_{\max} + \omega_{\min})}{2} = \frac{V}{c}\frac{1}{\cos\phi} \approx \frac{V}{c}. \tag{6}$$

Here we made use of the small-angle approximation $\cos(\phi) \approx 1$. This relation is applicable in the same range as the expansion for the tan function, and the error is also of the same magnitude.

In **Figure 14** we determine the interval from $\omega_0 - \Delta\omega/2$ to $\omega_0 + \Delta\omega/2$ and read off the interval of yarn tension it corresponds to. The amplitude of yarn tension oscillations is then simply the difference between the maximal and minimal values.

This graphical method for making estimations can be applied to better understand **Figure 15**, where we plot the dependence of the oscillation amplitude on the package radius for winding angle $\phi = 10°$ and unwinding velocity V = 2000 m/min. This is, in fact, a section of **Figure 13** at constant angle ϕ. As a rough rule, the amplitude of the oscillations decreases with increasing package radius c. In addition,

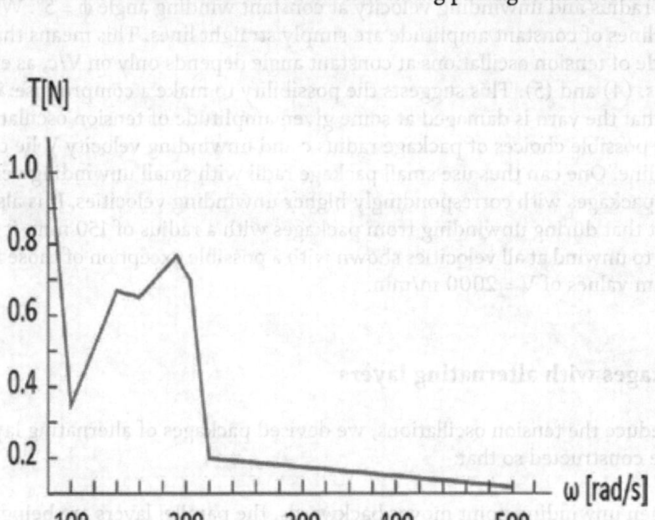

Figure 15.
Cross section of the plot at ϕ =10°.

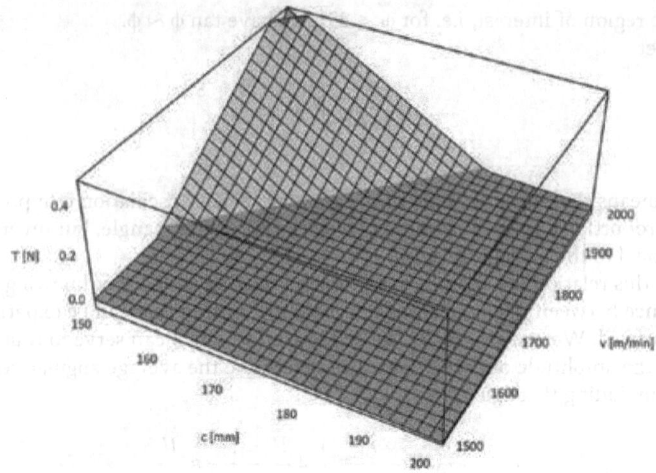

Figure 16.
Comparison of the amplitude of the tension oscillation as a function of the unwinding velocity V and the package radius c. The winding angle is constant, ϕ =5°.

however, one observes a peak in the range of radii from c = 110 to 180 mm. This is due to the particular dependence of the tension on the angular velocity, as shown in **Figure 14**. In some ranges of ω, this dependence is steeper, for instance, from ω = 200 to 240 rad/s. In this interval, oscillations of angular velocity lead to large amplitude of tension oscillations. In other ranges, for instance, from ω = 250 to 300 rad/s, the tension does not depend much on the angular velocity; hence the yarn tension oscillations are small.

The cross section of the previous figure at the winding angle ϕ =10°.

In **Figure 16** we plot the dependence of tension oscillation amplitude from the package radius and unwinding velocity at constant winding angle ϕ = 5°. We notice that the lines of constant amplitude are simply straight lines. This means that the amplitude of tension oscillations at constant angle depends only on V/c, as expected from Eqs. (4) and (5). This suggests the possibility to make a compromise: if it is known that the yarn is damaged at some given amplitude of tension oscillations, then the possible choices of package radius c and unwinding velocity V lie of a straight line. One can thus use small package radii with small unwinding velocities or large packages with correspondingly higher unwinding velocities. It is also apparent that during unwinding from packages with a radius of 150 mm, it is possible to unwind at all velocities shown with a possible exception of those near the maximum values of V = 2000 m/min.

4. Packages with alternating layers

To reduce the tension oscillations, we devised packages of alternating layers. They are constructed so that:

a. When unwinding point moves backwards, the parallel layers are being unwound.

b. When unwinding point moves forward, the layers with high winding angle are being unwound. Between two parallel layers, there should always be one layer with higher winding angle in order to avoid interweaving of parallel layers.

In **Figures 17** and **18**, we compare packages with alternating layers with regular cross-wound packages. The unwinding velocity is V = 2000 m/min for two package radii c = 200 and 150 mm. The winding angle of cross-wound layers is ϕ = 10°. As expected, the packages with alternating parallel-wound and cross-wound layers significantly reduce the tension. We have thus achieved an elimination of high tension spikes which lead to yarn breaking in conventional cross-wound packages. For this reason, the new-generation packages would allow unwinding at higher velocities than traditional packages.

In **Figures 19–21**, we compare the amplitude of the yarn tension oscillation in regular cross-wound packages and in new-generation packages for different unwinding velocities from V = 1000 to 2000 m/min and for different winding angles, from ϕ = 0 to 20°. Package radii are 120, 150, and 200 mm. The amplitude of tension oscillation is larger for large unwinding velocities and for larger winding angles. This is the case for all package radii. The totality of the results indicates that this dependence is significantly larger for conventional cross-wound packages,

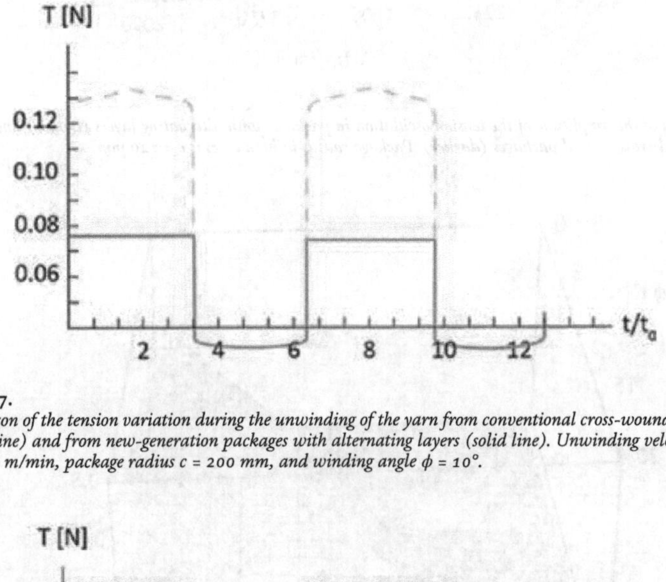

Figure 17.
Comparison of the tension variation during the unwinding of the yarn from conventional cross-wound packages (dashed line) and from new-generation packages with alternating layers (solid line). Unwinding velocity V = 2000 m/min, package radius c = 200 mm, and winding angle ϕ = 10°.

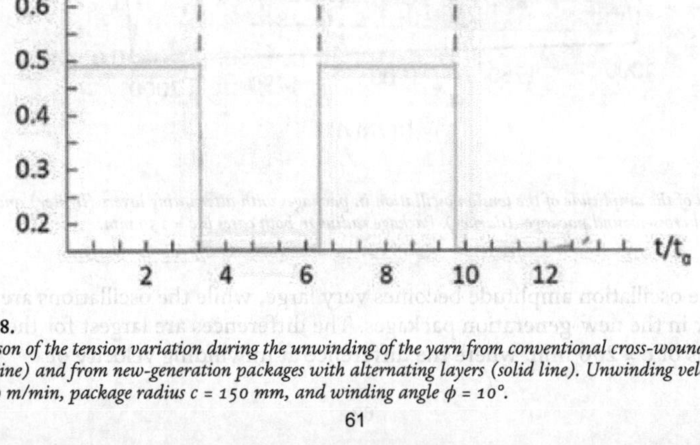

Figure 18.
Comparison of the tension variation during the unwinding of the yarn from conventional cross-wound packages (dashed line) and from new-generation packages with alternating layers (solid line). Unwinding velocity V = 2000 m/min, package radius c = 150 mm, and winding angle ϕ = 10°.

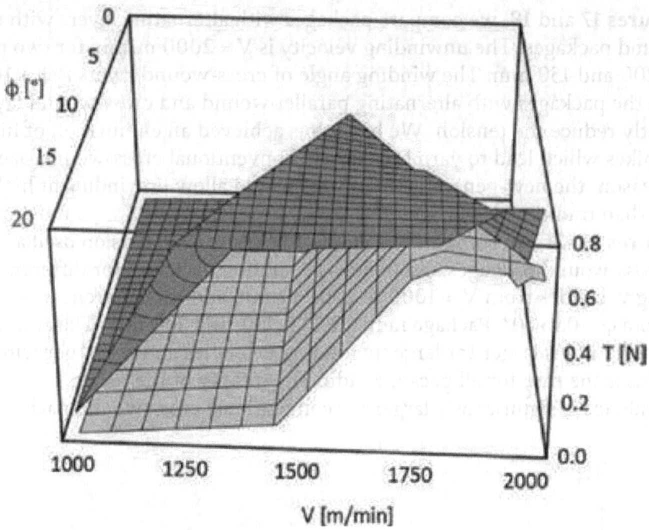

Figure 19.
Comparison of the amplitude of the tension oscillation in packages with alternating layers (lighter) and in conventional cross-wound packages (darker). Package radius in both cases is c = 120 mm.

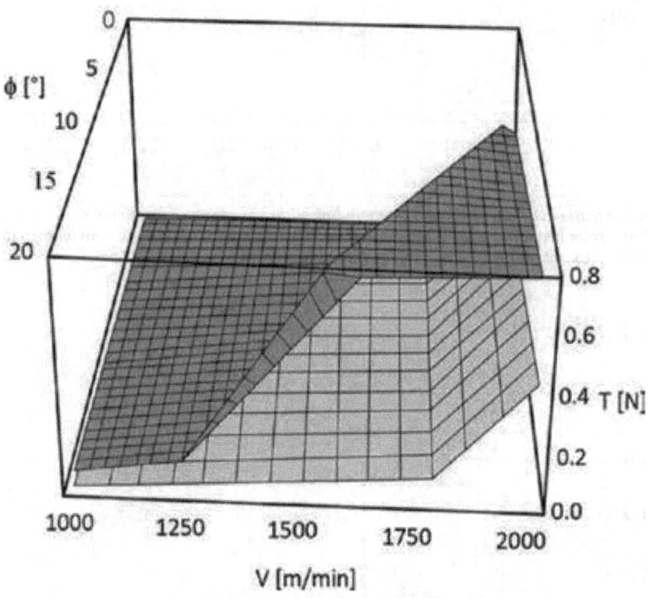

Figure 20.
Comparison of the amplitude of the tension oscillation in packages with alternating layers (lighter) and in conventional cross-wound packages (darker). Package radius in both cases is c = 150 mm.

where the oscillation amplitude becomes very large, while the oscillations are notably lower in the new-generation packages. The differences are largest for the package radius of c = 200 mm, where the difference at unwinding velocity of

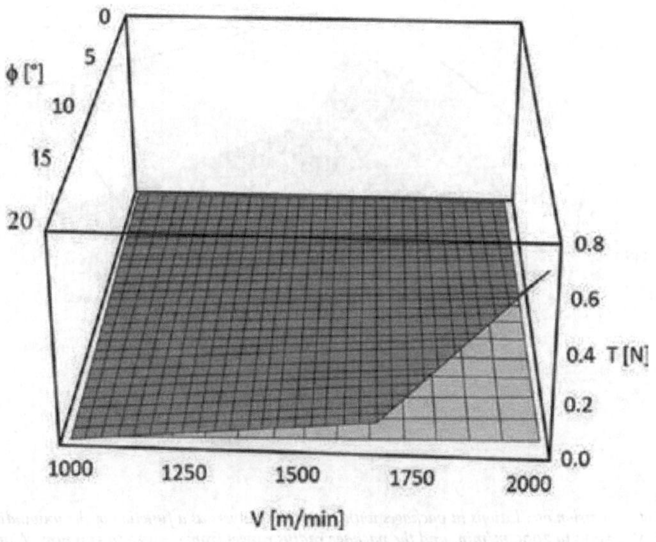

Figure 21.
Comparison of the amplitude of the tension oscillation in packages with alternating layers (lighter) and in conventional cross-wound packages (darker). Package radius in both cases is c = 200 mm.

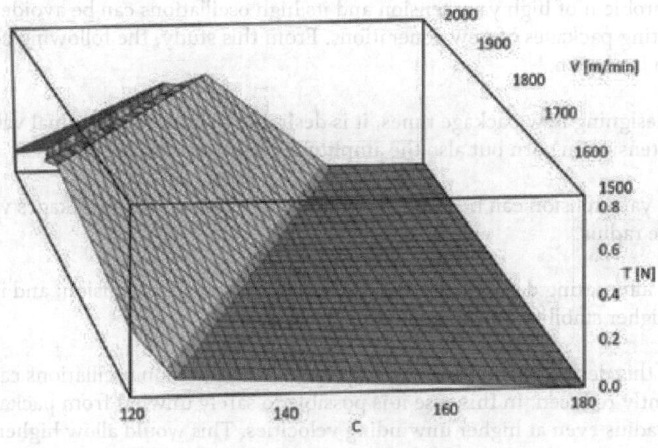

Figure 22.
Amplitude of the tension oscillations in packages with alternating layers as a function of the unwinding velocity ranges from V = 1500 to 2000 m/min, and the package radius ranges from c = 120 to 180 mm. Winding angle ϕ = 10°.

V = 2000 m/min equals 0.65 N. At package radius of c = 150 mm, this difference is still 0.4 cN.

In **Figures 22** and **23**, we show the amplitude of the tension oscillations in new-generation packages as a function of package radius and unwinding velocity at constant winding angle of cross-wound layers of ϕ = 10°. The first figure suggests that at V = 2000 m/min, the package radius should be at least c = 150 mm in order to avoid yarn breaking.

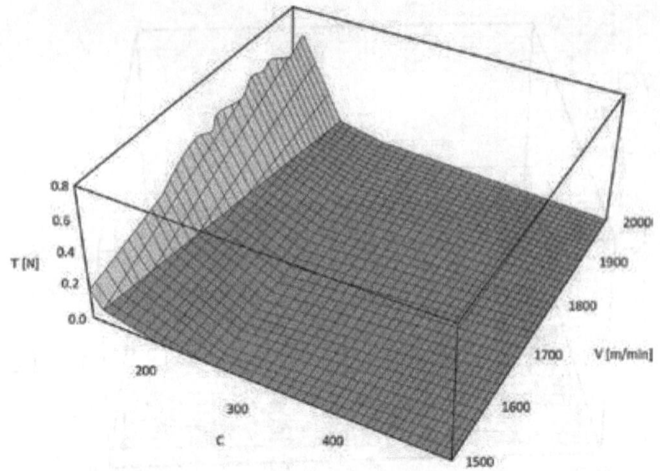

Figure 23.
Amplitude of the tension oscillations in packages with alternating layers as a function of the unwinding velocity ranges from V = 1000 to 2000 m/min, and the package radius ranges from c = 120 to 500 mm. Winding angle $\phi = 10°$.

5. Conclusion

The problem of high yarn tension and its high oscillations can be avoided by constructing packages of new generations. From this study, the following conclusions can be drawn:

- In designing new package times, it is desirable to limit the maximal value of the tension in yarn but also the amplitude of the tension oscillations.
- The yarn tension can be strongly reduced by making use of packages with large radius.
- The alternating design helps to reduce sudden change of tension, and it leads to higher stability of the unwinding process.

With this design tension and the amplitude of the tension oscillations can be significantly reduced. In this case it is possible to safely unwind from packages of smaller radius even at higher unwinding velocities. This would allow higher production rates without increased downtime due to yarn breaking. Based on the results of our calculations, we propose a package with the following characteristics: the inner cylinder radius should be 150 mm (arguably even 100 or 120 mm), and the outer package radius should be from 400 to 500 mm. Parallel layers should have a winding angle that is as close to 0 as possible, while the winding angle of other layers should be no higher than 10°.

References

[1] Kothari VK, Leaf GAV. The unwinding of yarns from packages. Part I: The theory of yarn-unwinding. Journal of the Textile Institute. 1979;**3**:89-95. DOI: 10.1080/00405007908631523

[2] Kothari VK, Leaf GAV. The unwinding of yarns from packages. Part II: Unwinding from cylindrical packages. Journal of the Textile Institute. 1979;**3**:96-104. DOI: 10.1080/00405007908631523

[3] Fraser WB, Ghosh TK, Batra SK. On unwinding yarn from cylindrical package. Proceedings of the Royal Society of London. 1992;**436**:479-498. DOI: 10.1080/rspa.1992.0030

[4] Fraser WB. The effect of yarn elasticity on an unwinding ballon. The Journal of The Textile Institute. 1992;**83**:603-613. DOI: 10.1080/00405009208631235

[5] Kong XM, Rahn CD, Goswami BC. Steady-state unwinding of yarn from cylindrical packages. Textile Research Journal. 1999;**69**(4):292-306. DOI: 10.1177/004051759906900040

[6] Clark JD, Fraser WB, Sharma R, Rahn CD. The dynamic response of a ballooning yarn: Theory and experiment. Proceedings of the Royal Society of London. 1998;**A454**: 2767-2789. DOI: 10.1098/rspa.1998.0280

[7] Praček S. Theory of string motion in the textile process of yarn unwinding. International Journal of Nonlinear Sciences and Numerical Simulation. 2007;**8**(3):451-460. DOI: 10.1515/IJNSNS.2007.8.3.415

[8] Pušnik N, Praček S. The effect of winding angle on unwinding yarn. Transactions of FAMENA. 2016;**40**(3): 29-42. DOI: 10.21278/TOF.40303. ISSN 1333–1124

Section 3

Technical Textiles Design and Development

Chapter 5

Stab Resistant Analysis of Body Armour Design Features Manufactured via Fused Deposition Modelling Process

Abstract

Five designs of imbricate scale armour features for stab-resistant application were printed via fused deposition modelling process. Stab test on these designs against the HOSDB KR1-E1 stab-resistant body armour standard with impact energy of 24 Joules was conducted. The stab test was conducted on a number of samples measured thicknesses ranging from 4.0 to 10.0 mm by using Instron CEAST 9340 Drop Impact Tower to determine a minimum thickness that resulted in a knife penetration through the underside of sample which does not exceed the maximum penetration permissibility of 7.0 mm. Materials used for the samples were ABS-M30 and PC-ABS. Finally, one of the designs which offered the highest knife penetration resistance was selected. The results show that PC-ABS samples provide less shattering and lower overall knife penetration depth in comparison with ABS-M30. PC-ABS stab test demonstrated a minimum thickness of 8.0 mm, which was the most adequate to be used in the development of FDM manufactured body armour design features. Lastly, the design feature of D5 has shown to exhibit the highest resistance to the knife penetration due to the penetration depth of 3.02 mm, which was the lowest compared to other design features.

Keywords: fused deposition modelling, stab resistant, body armour, design features

1. Introduction

Sharp force injury is a common threat that police officers encounter since they involve in a wide range of duties from general, daily, patrol activities to specific criminal activities such as narcotic investigation [1, 2]. Stab resistant body armour has been increasingly used by the law enforcement and corrections officers in the European and Asian countries where more likely involve violent knife crimes due to tight restrictions on gun ownership [3].

In the United States, data released by the Federal Bureau of Investigation have shown that the law enforcement officers killed by handgun, rifle and shotgun occupied the highest percentage from 2005 to 2014 [4]. About 0.4% of the law enforcement officers were killed by knife or other cutting instruments, as compared to other threats [4]. Despite the mortality rate caused by knife or other cutting tools was low, the stab resistant body armour has some practical and commercial experience in current service of the police forces [5].

The stab resistant body armour can be made from a range of materials, from traditional solutions, which are relatively heavy and provide little penetrate resistance, to the modern body armour made of ceramic, polycarbonate or aramid fibres which provide excellent stab protection, but are bulky, inflexible and uncomfortable to wear [6]. In an effort to reduce these limitations, the manufacture of stab resistant body armour must adhere to a series of internationally recognised test standards. According to the British HOSDB 2007 standard against knives and spikes, the knife should not penetrate more than 7 mm at the E1 press and 20 mm at the E2 press.

Besides, a number of studies were performed to reduce the weight of body armour and improve its flexibility. Stab resistance of modern armour was undoubtedly improved through implementation of modern standards, but historical issues such as comfort issues that causes thermal stress, poor fitting of armour hindering the body movement of wearers and affecting their work performance, etc. continue to exist with many of the current armour protection solutions [7, 8].

However, one of the alternative manufacturing technologies, the additive manufacturing (AM), has been increasingly implemented in a range of novel applications for customised clothing and high-performance textiles [9]. AM is an approach in which parts are designed in 3D CAD data and built by stacking material in layers [10]. AM technology allows the creation of complex geometries with reduced production time and cost, as well as the frequency of human intervention, which would be virtually difficult or impossible to produce via the traditional manufacturing processes such as injection moulding and milling. This technology presents an opportunity to design and develop novel solutions for conventional and high-performance textile applications because of their ability in generating geometric complexity and functionality as available from conventional fibre-based textiles [9]. Textile structures realised via AM techniques have received increasing attention since the previous decade. However, this solution is yet to be widely explored in an attempt to overcome the body armour issues. There are a range of AM techniques available in the market, including stereolithography apparatus (SLA), selective laser sintering (SLS), three-dimensional printing (3DP), and fused deposition modelling (FDM). However, FDM is the most widely used technique among these AM processes due to its simplicity and flexibility in manufacturing pure plastic parts with low cost, minimal wastage, and ease of material change [11, 12], which was first established by the Stratasys.

The world's first 3D conformal seamless AM textile garment was designed and manufactured by Bingham using Laser Sintering (LS) system [9]. The applications of AM textiles mostly via LS and 3D printer, especially in the field of fashion design, continue to increase. In addition, Johnson [13] attempted to address the issues that continue to exist with many current protective solutions in the body armour through AM. In their study, LS was adopted to develop stab resistant test samples for body armour. Browning [14] studied the structure of composite elasmoid type scales by measuring the mechanical response to blunt and penetrating indentation loading. In their study, additive manufactured model produced by using Fused Deposition Modelling technique was used only to mimic the feature of fish scale. However, there is no study about the creation of additive manufactured textiles via FDM system for stab resistant body protective armour with improved comfort ability and reduced weight.

2. Methodology

The aim of this research is to investigate the possibility of manufacturing stab resistant body armour samples via AM technology, specifically FDM. It is anticipated that the use of FDM can overcome the complexity in designing and manufacturing of stab resistant body armour, as well as reducing the weight and increasing the manoeuvrability of the body armour. The main objectives of the research are to investigate the feasibility of using FDM system to print the samples for stab resistance test; to design imbricated textile assembly with different design features; and to determine the results in terms of stab resistant performance under knife impact of 24 Joules according to the British HOSDB 2007 standard against knives and spikes impact.

2.1 Material used

Three stab tests were performed. Firstly, stab test was performed on planar samples measured thicknesses ranging from 4.0 to 6.0 mm, increasing in 1.0 mm increments fabricated with two different materials ABS-M30 and PC-ABS, respectively, in order to determine the most suitable material for the further stab resistance test and the stab resistant of this thickness range. Further stab test was performed on the selected material with higher range of thicknesses, which is from 7.0 to 10.0 mm, increasing in 1.0 mm increments mainly due to the previous thickness range that has failed to prevent the knife from being penetrated through the underside of the planar samples.

Furthermore, five different design features of the body armour were generated based on the combined knowledge of various design features which can be found in the natural biological body armour solutions such as animals and plants. In the end, one of the designs that provides the highest protection was selected—with the knife penetrated underneath the specimens was the lowest among all the designs. All five designs were designed mainly based on the inspiration of the hierarchal arrangement of elasmoid scales, which is regarded can offer high flexibility and provide multiple levels of protection to penetration [15, 16], as well as integrated with the design geometries of the other scales, as summarised in **Table 1**. Each scale assembly was formed via hinging connection features, which is inspired by the scale-based armour patents, in order to allow the scales to freely move among each other.

Table 2 shows the cross section of D1 which has been initially constructed with an assembly angle of 20°, while the individual scale thickness was 8.0 mm to ensure that minimum thickness established for the assembly was at least or not smaller than the minimum requirement of FDM printed sample—8.0 mm. Combining both thickness and assembly angle, a minimum cross-sectional thickness of 8.51 mm was achieved for D1. Scale thickness of D2 was reduced from 8.0 to 4.0 mm in an attempt to lower the total armour thickness and total assembly height of the following assemblies. Such reduction of scale thickness can be referred to the design features of elasmoid scales which informed that a scale thickness at the overlapping region is measured twice less than the thickness measured at the exposed region to form a multi-layered architecture [17]. To do this, the overlapping angle of individual scale element should be minimised to allow the formation of multi-layered overlapping layout. Browning [14] concluded that the scale armour featured imbricate scale assembly angle in between 10 and 20° able to offer higher flexibility and better protection due to the multi-layered structure and potentially to reduce back face deformation. The range of 10–20° assembly angle increasing 1° increments were therefore investigated, as shown in **Table 3**.

Design	Image	Description
D1	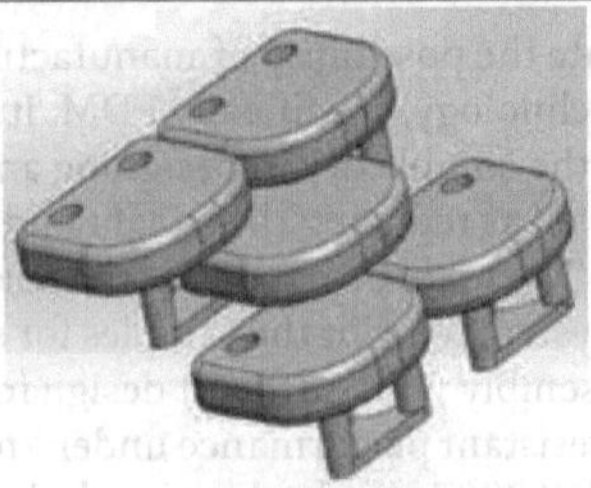	This design was generated based on the inspiration that combined the design features of both the ancient Roman Lorica Squamata, which mimicked the design of natural elasmoid scale armour to allow a greater movement between the scale elements and potentially offer a high mobility to the wearer.
D2	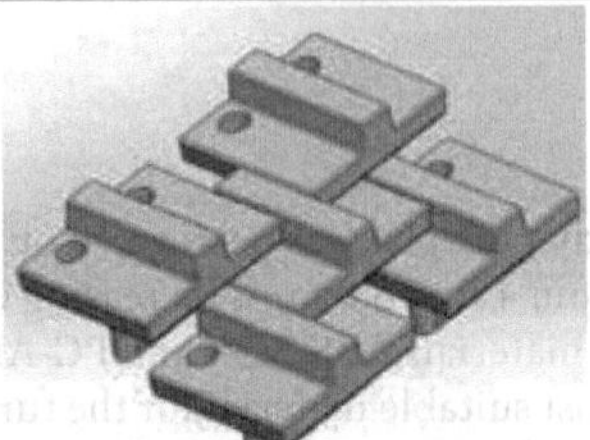	This design was constructed with a thickness of 4.0 mm base scale element featuring a central protrusion along the top surface of each scale element, which is inspired by the geometric characteristic of the placoid and osteoderms. The purpose of using such structural feature was to eliminate the weakness found in between the overlapped scale elements.
D3	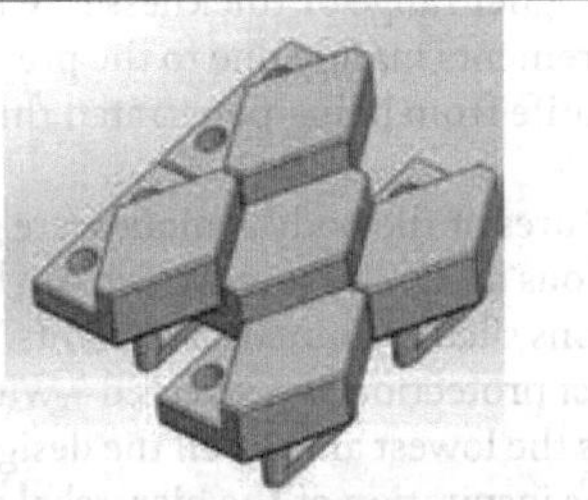	This design was created based on the design feature of elasmoid scale, which has different thicknesses at both overlapped and exposed regions. The exposed region of each planar scale was extruded with a hexagonal-shaped geometry from the top surface to encourage interlinking and manoeuvrability between individual elements and to assist in creating a multi-layered structure across the assembly.
D4	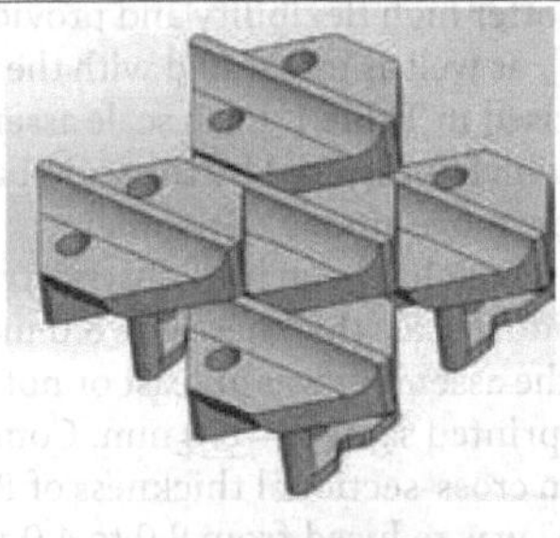	This design was designed with a thinner central protrusion along the top surface and gradually reducing closer to the edge of scales. Besides, an additional base plate extruded from the bottom of each scale element. Such design feature was inspired by combining the designs from both of the placoid scales and osteoderms, in order to eliminate the weakness found in between the overlapped scale element and, at the same time, to enhance the protective performance from all degrees.
D5	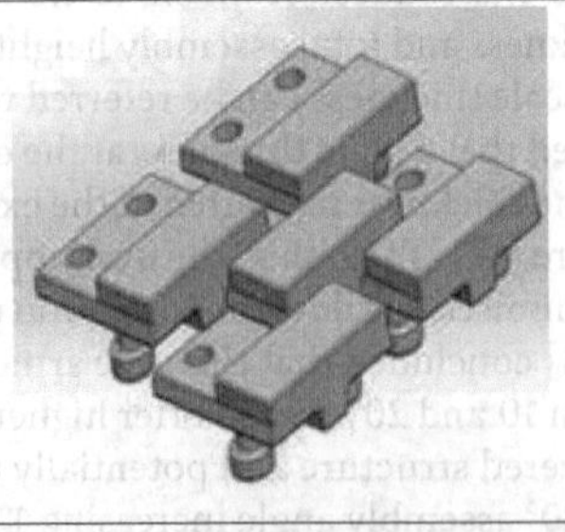	This design was designed in opposition to the idea of D4 by adding a wider central protrusion at the bottom part of each scale element and an additional rectangular plate on their top surfaces, in an attempt to resist the penetration of knife.

Table 1.
Comparisons of five different design features.

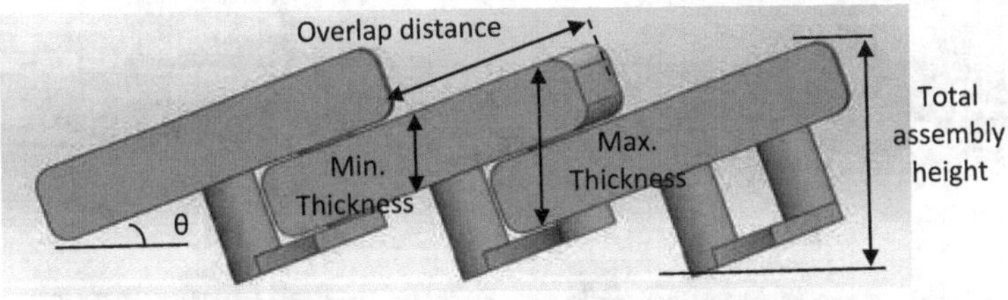

Assembly angle, θ (°)	Total assembly height (mm)	Overlap distance (mm)	Minimum thickness (mm)	Maximum thickness (mm)	Imbrications factor (K_d)
20	24.97	23.41	8.51	17.45	0.585

Table 2.
Cross section of D1.

Assembly angle (°)	Overlap distance (mm)	Minimum thickness (mm)	Maximum thickness (mm)	Imbrications factor (K_d)
20	12.09	11.34	13.62	0.302
19	12.78	8.88	13.54	0.320
18	13.54	8.83	13.46	0.339
17	14.39	8.78	13.38	0.360
16	15.34	8.74	13.33	0.384
15	16.42	8.70	13.25	0.411
14	17.65	8.66	13.19	0.441
13	19.06	8.62	8.62	0.465
12	20.70	4.09	8.59	0.518
11	22.64	4.07	8.56	0.566
10	24.95	4.06	8.53	0.624

Table 3.
Investigation of assembly angle at 10–20°.

Based on the investigation of each assembly angle, the assembly angle that does not provide the imbricate scale assembly a minimum of 8.0 mm thickness or above will not be further considered in developing the other designs. **Table 3** highlights that a minimum thickness of 8.62 mm was obtained at the assembly angle of 13°, which fulfilled the requirement of minimum 8.0 mm thickness. The maximum thickness for the assembly overlapped at this angle was also established at a value of 8.62 mm. Besides, armour samples that designed with this assembly angle should be able to provide higher protection than D1 since the imbrication factor (K_d) was lower. **Figure 1** shows the section views of all designs, stab points, minimum thicknesses and total heights.

All the test samples were manufactured via Stratasys Fortus 400 MC which can provide higher quality of products. **Figure 2** shows the examples of PC-ABS material planar samples, and **Figure 3** shows the imbricate scale armour that was printed. It has to be noted that the creation of all designs must be considered on the FDM design guide to avoid part failure when building with FDM system. **Table 4**

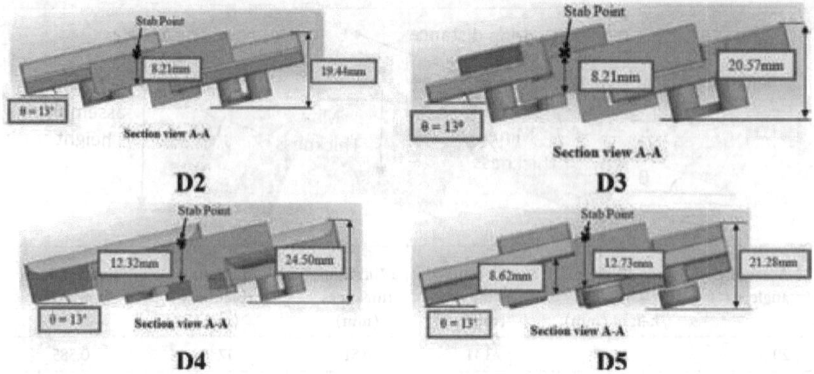

Figure 1.
Section view of all designs.

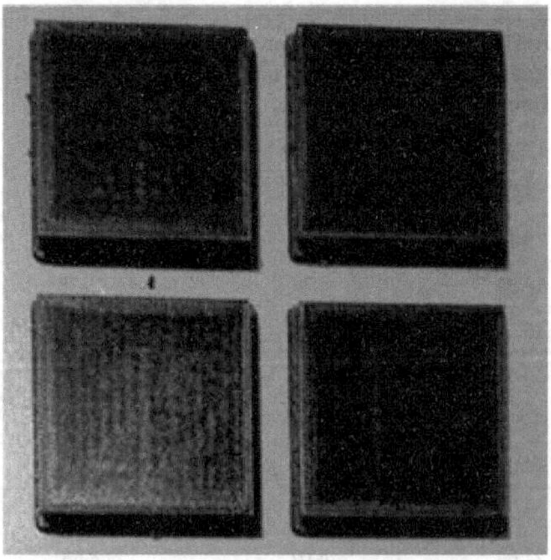

Figure 2.
Planar sample.

shows the process parameters used in printing the test samples. Both planar and imbricate test samples were printed with solid part interior fill to avoid from easily being penetrated by the knife. These samples were also built in 0° orientation and with wall thickness, that is, more than twice the layer thickness, in order to produce samples that have higher strength and impact resistance, and at the same time to minimise the height of printing which will affect the build time. However, build parameters such as raster angle, raster width and air gap, applied for both the materials were set to the default value.

Stab test was conducted using Instron CEAST 9340 Drop Tower (**Figure 4**) and securely installed with HOSDB standardised knife blade which dropped in the same direction of gravity during the stab test. By considering this, the stab test was performed at HOSDB KR1 with stab impact energy at E1 in the research; the acceptable blade penetration protruding through the underside of each test sample must not exceed a maximum penetration of 7.0 mm. In order to fulfil the requirements at this stab energy level, the parameters that include drop height and drop velocity need to be determined prior the stab test, as summarised in **Table 5**. Additionally, all these tests were conducted under an ambient temperature of 23°C with a relative humidity of 50%.

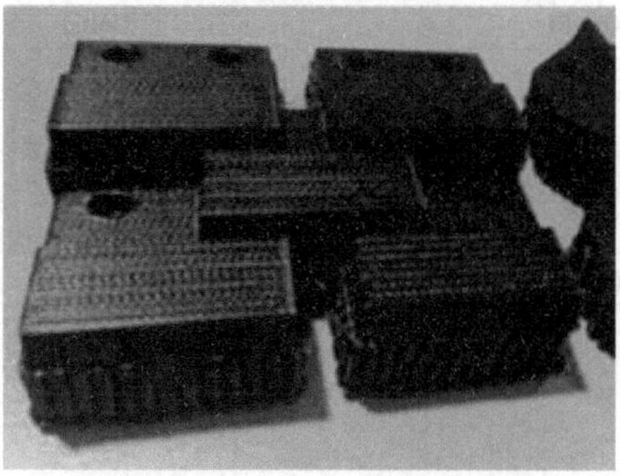

Figure 3.
Imbricate sample.

Parameters	Unit	ABS-M30	PC-ABS
Layer thickness	mm	0.254	0.254
Tip size	mm	T16	T16
Raster angle	°	45	45
Raster width	mm	0.014	0.014
Air gap	mm	0	0
Fill	%	100	100
Maximum build temperature	°C	325	335
Filament colour	—	white	black

Table 4.
Build parameters for ABS-M30 and PC-ABS materials.

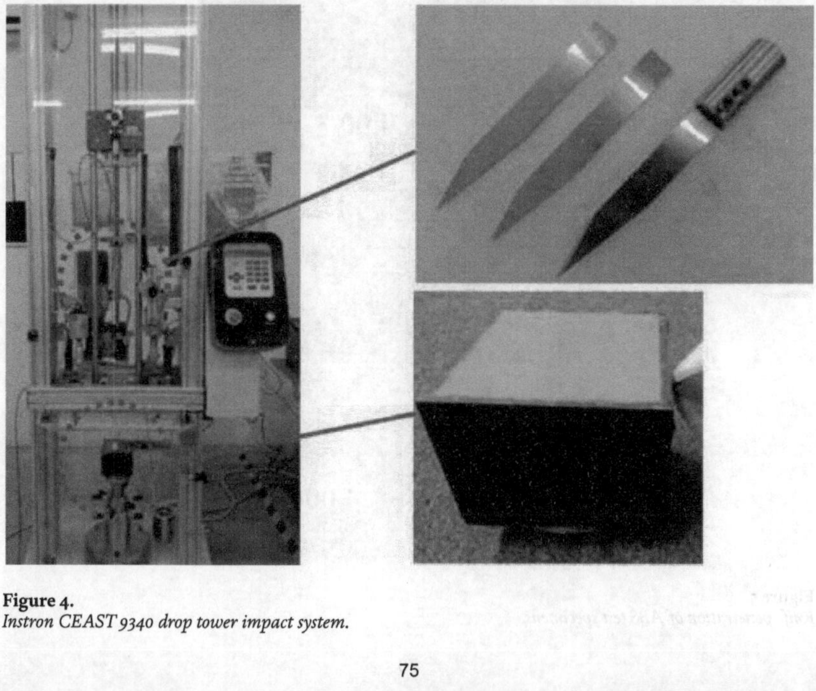

Figure 4.
Instron CEAST 9340 drop tower impact system.

Test requirements at KR1-E1	Units	Value settings
Stab impact energy	Joules	24 ± 0.5
Total drop mass	kg	3.226
Drop height	m	0.758
Drop velocity	m/s	3.86
Maximum blade penetration	mm	7.0

Table 5.
Experimental requirements of stab test at KR1-E1.

3. Results and discussion

Knife penetration depth occurred within the ABS-M30 and PC-ABS specimens measured with thickness groups ranging from 4.0 to 6.0 mm were significantly higher than the maximum allowable penetration of 7.0 mm, which indicates that this range was not suitable to be used for further armour designs. For ABS-30, samples measured with thicknesses of 4.0 and 5.0 mm were shattered into two pieces (**Figure 5**) and allowed a deep blade penetration into the backing clay. The measurement of knife penetration through the underside of these specimens was unpredictable since the samples were broken into pieces. However, the 5.00/3 sample was only punctured by the knife blade and caused a piece of small fragment broken from the underside of the specimen with a knife penetration depth of 20.10 mm, as documented in **Table 6**. The knife blade punctured through the 6.0 mm thick specimens does not cause any shatter to the sample, however the penetration depth occurred in the 6.00/3 sample was measured as 6.32 mm which has satisfied the allowable limit of knife penetration depth as defined in the HOSDB KR1-E1. The knife blade has pierced through the specimen and caused the underside

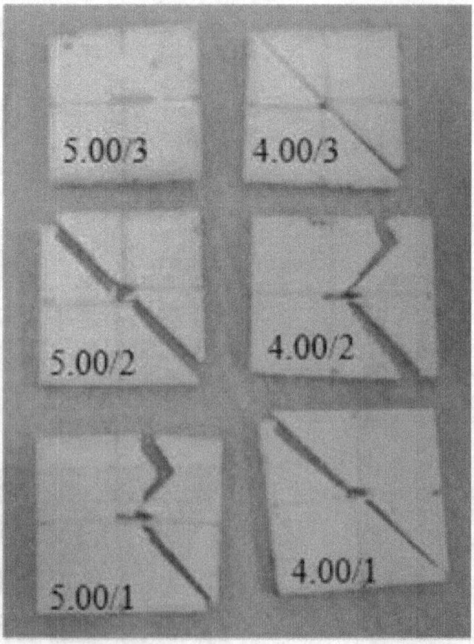

Figure 5.
Knife penetration of ABS test specimens.

Test	Specimen ID	Failure mode	Penetration depth (mm)	Result
1	6.00/1	Punctured	13.30	Fail
2	6.00/2	Punctured	9.65	Fail
3	6.00/3	Punctured	6.32	Pass
4	5.00/1	Shattered	—	Fail
5	5.00/2	Shattered	—	Fail
6	5.00/3	Punctured	20.10	Fail
7	4.00/1	Shattered	—	Fail
8	4.00/2	Shattered	—	Fail
9	4.00/3	Shattered	—	Fail

Table 6.
Stab test result of ABS-M30 test specimens.

Test	Specimen ID	Failure mode	Penetration depth (mm)	Result
1	6.00/1	Punctured	14.96	Fail
2	6.00/2	Punctured	16.08	Fail
3	6.00/3	Punctured	15.23	Fail
4	5.00/1	Punctured	21.88	Fail
5	5.00/2	Punctured	20.06	Fail
6	5.00/3	Punctured	21.07	Fail
7	4.00/1	Punctured	39.40	Fail
8	4.00/2	Shattered	—	Fail
9	4.00/3	Shattered	—	Fail

Table 7.
Stab test result of PC-ABS test specimens.

of specimen to crack from the stabbed region. However, it has to be noted that all the three 6.0 mm thick ABS-M30 specimens were forced deeply into the backing clay as compared to the other thickness group samples.

Table 7 shows the knife penetration depth measured from the underside surface of the PC-ABS planar samples measured thicknesses ranging from 4.0 to 6.0 mm. All samples failed to withstand the knife penetration since all the recorded penetration depth were higher than the maximum permissibility of 7.0 mm. However, total cases of shattering occurred in the PC-ABS were much less than the ABS-M30 since only two of the 4.0 mm thick PC-ABS samples (**Figure 6**) were shattered and demonstrated unmeasurable knife penetration.

Mean knife penetration depth of 6.0 mm thick ABS-M30 specimens was significantly lower than the PC-ABS specimens, with a difference of 5.67 mm, in spite of the mean knife penetrations occurred in both 6.0 mm thick ABS-M30 and PC-ABS samples were higher than the maximum permissibility of 7.0 mm. In that case, the stab resistance of the materials was further determined through the force/displacement traces of the impact event, and kinetic energy absorbed by the target samples measured 6.0 mm. **Figure 7** demonstrated the force/displacement traces of the impact event on the ABS-30 and PC-ABS target samples measured with thickness of 6.0 mm, respectively. The peak force values for the PC-ABS specimens in sequence order were approximately 0.992 kN, 0.918 kN and 0.987 kN, respectively, whereas

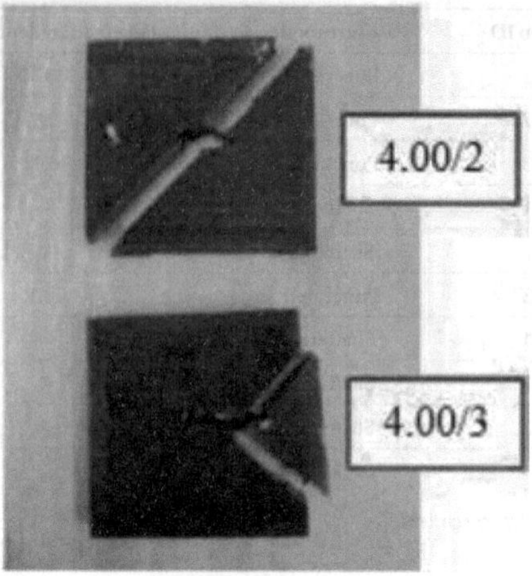

Figure 6.
Knife penetration of 4.00 mm test specimens.

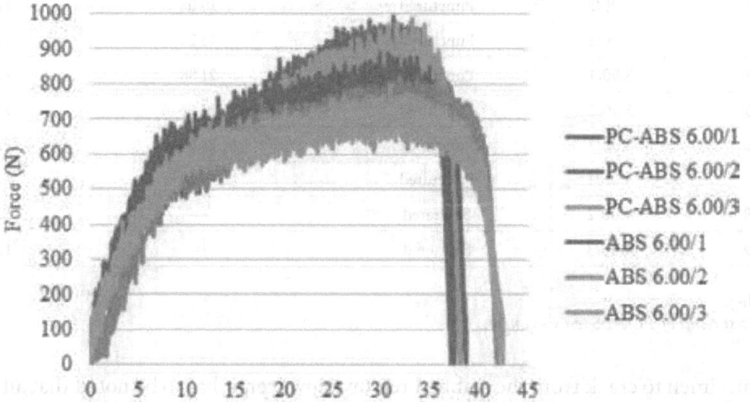

Figure 7.
Force/displacement traces.

the peak forces occurred in the ABS specimens were 0.890 kN, 0.822 kN and 0.800 kN, respectively. The force/displacement curves reveal that the maximum value of impact load where the failure of PC-ABS specimens began were higher than the ABS-M30 specimens. Besides, it can be also noted that the ABS-M30 specimens supported the load with longer displacement before completely penetrated as compared to the case of PC-ABS.

Impact damage in the FDM manufactured samples is caused by the loss of kinetic energy of the knife blade during penetration, so the energy absorption by the target specimens can be analysed using the formula, $E_{ab} = \frac{1}{2}m(v_i^2 - v_f^2)$, where E_{ab} is the energy absorbed by the target model during knife impact, m is the mass of the knife and v_i and v_f is referred to the initial and final velocity of the knife penetration [18]. **Figure 8** illustrated the energy absorbed by the ABS-M30 and PC-ABS specimens featured with 6.0 mm thickness group.

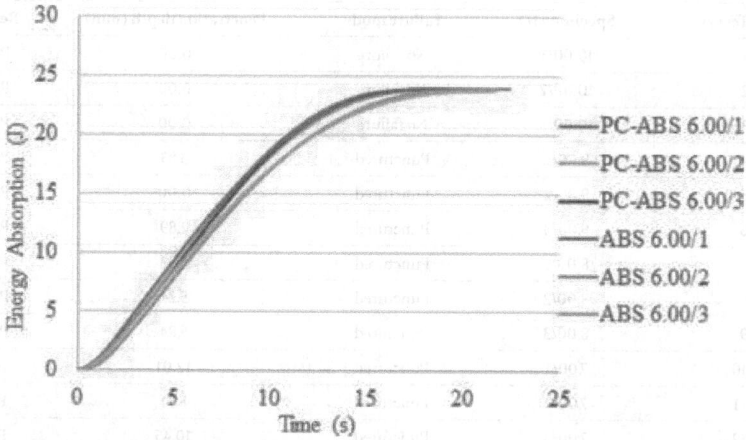

Figure 8.
Energy absorption by specimens measuring 6.00 mm thickness.

According to the trend shown in **Figure 8**, the ABS-M30 samples absorbed total energies of 23.967, 23.955 and 23.797 Joules, respectively, whereas the energy absorptions by the PC-ABS samples were 23.933, 23.950 and 23.948 Joules, respectively, which all were almost same as the available energy. Although the sample 6.00/1 of ABS-M30 material appeared to absorb higher stab impact energy than the PC-ABS samples, however, the overall mean energy absorption by the ABS-M30 specimens was slightly lower compared to the PC-ABS. On the whole, the PC-ABS tends to offer higher stab resistance performance than the ABS-M30 against the HOSDB KR1 E1 impact energy of 24 Joules. In addition, PC-ABS material tends to lock onto the knife blade to prevent it from being further penetrated, while the knife blade was also difficult to be released from the stabbed specimens. This can be attributed to the fracture toughness and impact resistance of PC-ABS; therefore, higher stab impact energy is required to pierce and deform it as compared to the ABS-M30 [19, 20].

PC-ABS planar specimens were then further constructed with thicknesses ranging from 7.0 to 10.0 mm and stab tested under the similar test conditions as previous experiment. The results obtained from this experiment were outlined within **Table 8**. Knife penetration through the underside surface of 7.0 mm thick PC-ABS samples was significantly higher than the maximum permissibility of 7.0 mm. However, the result obtained for 8.0 mm thick specimens was significantly reduced to an average depth of 5.47 mm which fulfilled the standard requirement. Furthermore, the samples measured thickness of 9.0 mm were only slightly punctured and resulted with a mean knife penetration depth of 2.24 mm. The samples measuring such thickness have demonstrated only one strike without knife punctured through the underside of the specimen. However, all of the 10.0 mm thick specimens resulted with no knife penetrated beyond the underside surfaces.

Figure 9 shows that the thickness of PC-ABS samples which was smaller than 8.0 mm provided lack of protection against the knife threat at this level, and it can be observed that the knife penetration depth was reduced as the thickness of samples increases, which indicates that the stab resistance increases as the thickness increases. Nevertheless, the thicknesses of 9.0 and 10.0 mm were not recommended to use for the further design activity of body armour via the FDM technique. Although these thicknesses provided higher stab resistance than

Test	Specimen ID	Failure mode	Penetration depth (mm)	Result
1	10.00/1	No failure	0.00	Pass
2	10.00/2	No failure	0.00	Pass
3	10.00/3	No failure	0.00	Pass
4	9.00/1	Punctured	3.83	Pass
5	9.00/2	Punctured	0.00	Pass
6	9.00/3	Punctured	2.89	Pass
7	8.00/1	Punctured	5.32	Pass
8	8.00/2	Punctured	5.24	Pass
9	8.00/3	Punctured	5.84	Pass
10	7.00/1	Punctured	12.01	Fail
11	7.00/2	Punctured	8.11	Fail
12	7.00/3	Punctured	10.45	Fail

Table 8.
Knife penetration depth of PC-ABS planar specimens.

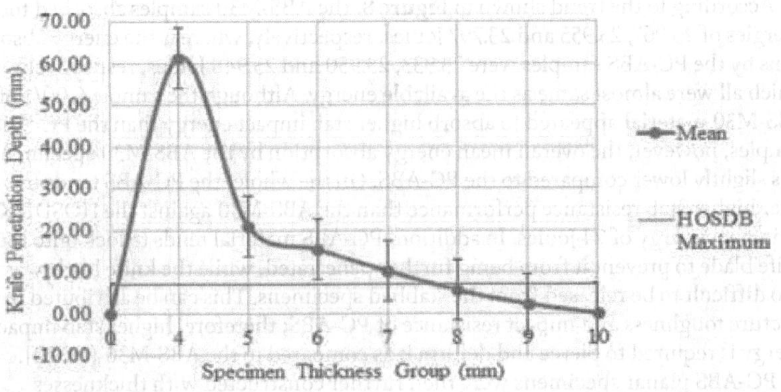

Figure 9.
Mean knife penetration depth per thickness group of PC-ABS planar specimens.

the thickness of 8.0 mm, but the concern was to avoid more weight added to the designs of body armour [21, 22]. Therefore, the 8.0 mm thickness was used as the minimum requirement in generating the designs of imbricate armour features.

Based on the result obtained in the stab test of the five designs, most of the stab tests demonstrated successful stab resistance which satisfied the requirement of lower than 7.0 mm, as defined within the HOSDB KR1-E1 impact energy of 24 Joules. However, the D2 and D3 demonstrated negative results to such level of impact energy, as demonstrated in **Figure 10**.

D3 offered the lowest stab resistance with a knife penetration depth which was the highest as compared to the other designs. The mean knife penetration depth was 12.08 mm which was larger than the HOSDB maximum penetration level. The minimum overlapping thickness where the knife punctured was the reason that caused the failure in D3 samples since it measured only 8.21 mm (**Figure 1**), which can be considered as the lowest measurement as compared to

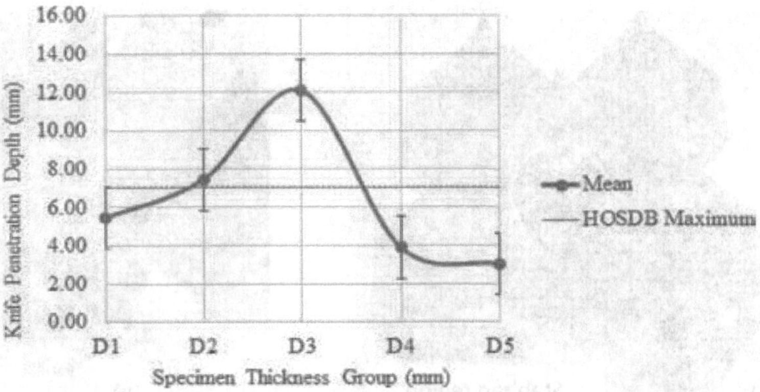

Figure 10.
Comparison of mean knife penetration depth of the design features.

other designs. Mean knife penetration depth resulted in D2 was 7.43 mm, which was lower than D3, but D2 did not effectively withstand the knife threat due to the knife penetration depth occurred in it was higher than 7.0 mm. On the other hand, D1, D4 and D5 demonstrated higher stab resistance to the HOSDB KR1-E1 impact energy. On the other hand, D1 provided acceptable level of protection with a mean knife penetration of 5.37 mm which was lower than 7.0 mm. However, this design was not as efficient as the designs of D4 and D5. This indicated that reduction in the total thickness of the imbricate structure will not reduce the stab resistance of the FDM-manufactured imbricate body armour, yet it can also provide more effective protection to the wearer from sustaining a life-threatening injury. Furthermore, D4 demonstrated stab resistance which was relatively lower than D5, since the mean knife penetration depth of the D4 specimens was 0.87 mm higher than that resulted in the D5 samples. **Figure 11** shows the test result of D4 specimen.

However, D5 samples demonstrated were most successful to withstand a knife threat to the HOSDB KR1 impact energy of 24 Joules since D5 has provided the highest stab resistance with a mean knife penetration depth of 3.02 mm which was the lowest as compared to the other designs. An individual scale was broken away from the D5 assembly as shown in **Figure 12** for illustration.

One of the reasons that causes the neighbour scale to be disconnected from the assembly was the design feature of assembly link which offered less effort to hold the scales tightly. Furthermore, the resistance between the knife blade and specimens has led to the formation of crack from the edges of the target scale. Despite one of the neighbour scales was disconnected from the assembly due to the impact of knife blade, the design feature of the assembly was able to lock the knife blade to resist further penetration into the structure of material. In addition, the stab resistance of the D5 will slightly reduce if the knife blade punctures at the front part which far away from the higher thickness region since thickness along the front part of sample was measured 8.62 mm (**Figure 1**). Despite the linkage failure occurred within D5 samples, the broken and loose pieces will be contained within the structure due to the overlapping nature of imbricate design. This may be not obviously seen in this experiment as the sample was not a complete body armour assembly. More importantly, this phenomenon has not resulted with knife penetration which is greater than the allowable limit of 7.0 mm and it was also the lowest among the designs.

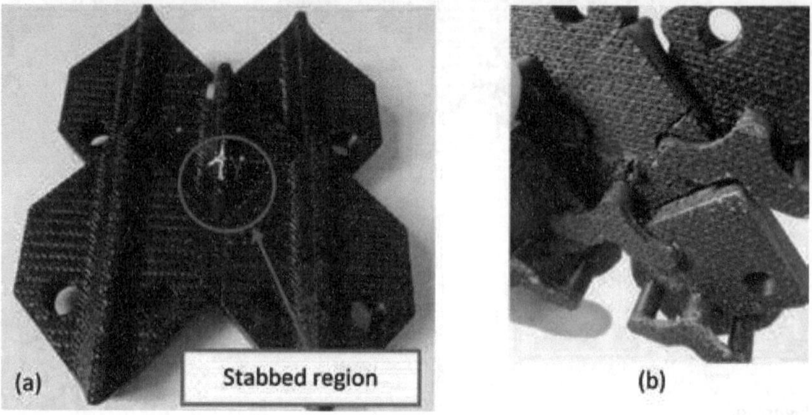

Figure 11.
Stab test result of D4 specimen from (a) top and (b) bottom view.

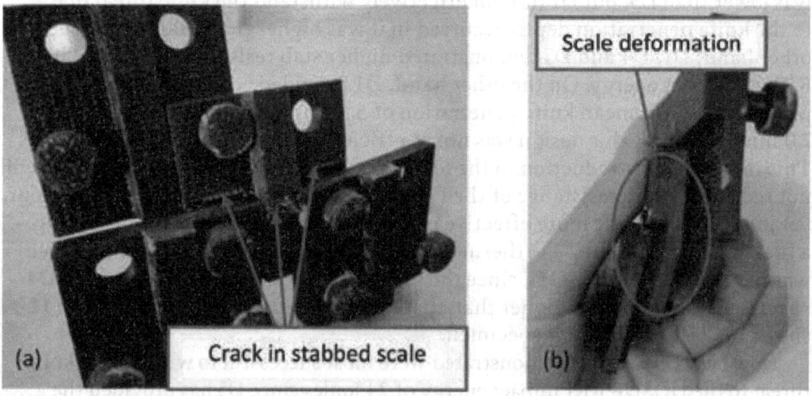

Figure 12.
Stab test result of D5 specimen from (a) bottom and (b) side view.

4. Conclusion

Stab experimental test was conducted on a range of planar specimens manufactured via Stratasys Fortus 400 MC system against HOSDB KR1-E1 impact energy of 24 Joules, to decide the selection of material and identify a minimum thickness of the FDM-manufactured specimens. It was important to identify the minimum thickness of the FDM-manufactured specimens for stab resistance, since the minimum thickness was necessary to provide a reference for the design of imbricate armour features. The result obtained in the stab test of the planar specimens demonstrated that the PC-ABS exhibited higher resistance to the knife blade due to the knife penetration depth that occurred in it was lower than the ABS-M30. Besides, less specimens manufactured from PC-ABS were shattered as compared with the PC-ABS; thus, the PC-ABS samples demonstrated higher levels of toughness and were therefore able to absorb the stab impact energy. Meanwhile, an optimum minimum thickness of 8.0 mm has been determined for specimens manufactured using PC-ABS. Although thicknesses of 9.0 and 10.0 mm have shown greater stab resistance than the 8.0 mm specimens, these thicknesses should not be used to establish the imbricate armour design features since it can increase the weight of armour.

Result obtained from the stab test has shown that the D5 design features which adopted an extruded plate at the exposed region of overlapping scales and featured a central protrusion along the bottom of each scales demonstrated the highest stab resistance against the knife penetration with an impact energy of 24 Joules as compared to the other designs. The knife penetration depth measured from this design was only 3.02 mm. Despite one of the neighbour scales was disconnected from the assembly due to the impact of knife blade, the design feature of the assembly was able to lock the knife blade to resist further penetration into the structure of material.

References

[1] Parsons JRL. 'Occupational Health and Safety Issues of Police Officers in Canada, the United States and Europe: A Review Essay' [Online]. 2004. Available at: https://www.mun.ca/safetynet/library/OHandS/OccupationalHS.pdf [Accessed on: 15 May 2018]

[2] National Institute of Justice. 'Stab Resistance of Personal Body Armor NIJ Standard–0115.00 (NCJ #183652). Rockville, MD: National Law Enforcement and Corrections Technology Center, U.S. Department of Justice; 2000

[3] Hilal SM, Densley JA, Li SD, Ma Y. The routine of mass murder in China. Homicide Studies. 2014;**18**(1):83-104

[4] Federal Bureau of Investigation. 2014 Preliminary Statistics for Law Enforcement Officers Killed and Assaulted [Online]. 2015. Available: https://ucr.fbi.gov/leoka/2014

[5] Horsfall I. 'Stab resistant body armour' [Ph.D. dissertation]. Cranfield: Cranfield University; 2000

[6] Egres Jr., RG, Decker MJ, Halbach CJ, Lee YS, Kirkwood JE, Kirkwood KM, et al. "Stab resistance of shear thickening fluid (STF) – Kevlar composites for bodyarmor applications". In: Proceedings of the 24th army science conference. Orlando, Florida; Nov. 29-Dec. 2. 2004

[7] Stubbs D, David G, Woods V, Beards S. Problems associated with police equipment carriage with body armour, including driving. In: Proceedings of the International Conference on Contemporary Ergonomics (CE2008). Nottingham, UK; 1-3 April 2008

[8] Xiong H. 'Police officers: Surviving a real life-threatening incident while wearing body armor' [Ph.D. thesis]. Stanislaus: California State University; 2014

[9] Bingham GA, Hague RJM, Tuck CJ, Long AC, Crookston JJ, Sherburn MN. Rapid manufactured textiles. International Journal of Computer Integrated Manufacturing. 2007;**20**(1):96-105

[10] Gibson I, Rosen D, Stucker B. Additive Manufacturing Technologies: 3D Printing, Rapid Prototyping, and Direct Digital Manufacturing. Berlin: Springer; 2014

[11] Ning F, Cong W, Qiu J, Wei J, Wang S. Additive manufacturing of carbon fiber reinforced thermoplastic composites using fused deposition modeling. Composites Part B: Engineering. 2015;**80**:369-378

[12] Chohan JS, Singh R. Pre and post processing techniques to improve surface characteristics of FDM parts: A state of art review and future applications. Rapid Prototyping Journal. 2017;**23**(3):495-513

[13] Johnson A, Bingham GA, Wimpenny DI. Additive manufactured textiles for high performance stab resistant applications. Rapid Prototyping Journal. 2013;**19**(3):199-207

[14] Browning A, Ortiz C, Boyce MC. Mechanics of composite elasmoid fish scale assemblies and their bioinspired analogues. Journal of the Mechanical Behavior of Biomedical Materials. 2013;**19**:75-86

[15] Helfman GS, Collette BB, Facey DE, Bowen BW. The Diversity of Fishes: Biology, Evolution, and Ecology. 2nd ed. New Jersey: John Wiley & Sons; 2009

[16] Zhu D, Ortega CF, Motamedi R, Szewciw L, Vernerey F, Barthelat F. Structure and mechanical

performance of a "Modern" fish scale. Advanced Engineering Materials. 2012;**14**(4):B185-B194

[17] Lin YS, Wei CT, Olevsky EA, Meyers MA. Mechanical properties and the laminate structure of arapaima gigas scales. Journal of the Mechanical Behavior of Biomedical Materials. 2011;**4**(7):1145-1156

[18] Dhakal HN, Zhang ZY, Richardson MOW, Errajhi OAZ. The low velocity impact response of non-woven hemp fibre reinforced unsaturated polyester composites. Composite Structures. 2007;**81**(4):559-567

[19] Seelig T, Van der Giessen E. Effects of microstructure on crack tip fields and fracture toughness in PC/ABS polymer blends. International Journal of Fracture. 2007;**145**(3):205-222

[20] Stratasys. 'FDM Thermoplastics Material Overview' [Online]. 2017. Available at: http://www.stratasys.com/materials/fdm [Accessed: 11 May 2018]

[21] Potter AW, Karis AJ, Gonzalez JA. 'Biophysical Characterization and Predicted Human Thermal Responses to US Army Body Armor Protection Levels (BAPL) (No. USARIEM-TR-T13-5)'. MA: U.S. Army Research Institute of Environmental Medicine. 2013

[22] Bossi LL, Jones ML, Kelly A, Tack DW. A Preliminary Investigation of the Effect of Protective Clothing Weight, Bulk and Stiffness on Combat Mobility Course Performance. Proceedings of the Human Factors and Ergonomics Society Annual Meeting. 2016;**60**(1):702-706

Index